Transportation
GIS

LAURA LANG

ESRI PRESS

Published by
Environmental Systems Research Institute, Inc.
380 New York Street
Redlands, California 92373-8100

Environmental Systems Research Institute, Inc.

Transportation GIS

ISBN 1-879102-47-1

Contents

Preface

In a typical day, Americans are on the road an hour and thirteen minutes, much of that time stuck in heavy traffic. Surprisingly, they actually log more than nine billion miles in that day. And the Federal Highway Agency (FHWA) expects highway use to increase some 50 percent by 2010. Whether that use will be travel or gridlock remains to be seen.

The choice looks clear. We build more and more roads for more and more cars and produce more and more pollution. Or, we stop driving so much. Fortunately for our health, the cost of just maintaining the roads and bridges we already have may be too much for most transportation department budgets. The FHWA estimates that we will have to spend 15 percent more each year just to maintain our highways and bridges in their current condition.

But many agencies of mass transit have found that with the right tools, the conflicting needs of people to move and to breathe can both be met. One of those tools, geographic information systems (GIS), is becoming more and more familiar to the nation's policy makers, planners, analysts, and researchers as the best way to assess traffic congestion, traffic safety, and air quality.

GIS helps them view all kinds of information, even create models that forecast the results of a project—building a new road, adding another bus route, or expanding the capacity of a bridge—all before time and money have been committed to it.

GIS is also useful in such programs as welfare-to-work for showing the transportation options available to people in low-income households.

The money this nation spends to improve our transportation infrastructure must offer long-term dividends, adding to the economic, social, and environmental health of its communities. With GIS, a versatile tool set for viewing all sides of an issue, we can design and build a transportation network we can all live with.

Jack Dangermond
President, ESRI

Acknowledgments

After attending the 1998 ESRI User Conference, which had standing-room-only attendance at transportation sessions, I realized it would be pretty easy to find enough user sites to fill a book with great applications of ArcView GIS, SDE, ARC/INFO, and MapObjects software; the real challenge would lie in selecting only twelve.

Ernie Ott, ESRI's transportation manager, helped me choose the best applications and, as the book was being written, assisted with coordination of graphics and reviews. Throughout this project, Ernie provided guidance, insight, and, most important, inspiration, and I am grateful to him for the faith he showed in me and for providing such excellent examples from his market.

Each organization we focused on had a compelling story to tell, showing how transportation projects, from airport design to highway maintenance, benefit from GIS. The people listed at the end of each chapter all spent countless hours giving interviews and responding to follow-up questions, preparing graphics, and reviewing drafts. This process took many months and their patience and perseverance are greatly appreciated.

Michael Karman edited chapters as they were written, conveying concepts more clearly and improving transitions. Michael Hyatt handled page design and production, as well as copyediting and proofreading chores. Lisa Godin assisted with editing and page layout. Gina Davidson designed and produced the cover, and Steve Pablo edited images. Barbara Shaeffer reviewed the text from a legal perspective, while Cliff Crabbe oversaw print production.

Thanks to the management team of ESRI Press—Christian Harder, Judy Boyd, and Bill Miller—for giving me the opportunity to write this book. And special thanks to Jack Dangermond for allocating the requisite resources to get *Transportation GIS* into the hands of transportation professionals everywhere.

Chapter 1

●●●●●● On the move

Walk into any store in your neighborhood and count the number of items that have come from only 5 or 6 miles away. Not many. Most come from dozens, hundreds, or thousands of miles away. Many come from halfway around the world. That means those items have been on trucks, planes, and then trucks again, and possibly in holds of ships or the freight cars of trains before they got to the store. Then they go home with you in a car, bus, or train.

And while more and more people are hooking up computers so they can work at home, most of us still drive to work. Even if we work at home, we still drive to the store and the theater, we still fly across the country to visit relatives, or across one ocean or another to snap photos of exotic places, eat exotic foods, and meet new and interesting people.

Mile after mile

All this traveling takes an enormously complex infrastructure—roads, runways, rails, harbors, docks, bridges, overpasses, signs, signals, fences, railings—mile after mile of them, in crowded cities and empty countrysides, through pitiless deserts and snowbound mountains, along hurricane-wracked coastlines, and through fault-ridden valleys.

Pounded and smashed by trucks and cars, lashed by wind and snow, everything in the whole system is used and abused, and everything in the whole system needs constant attention to stay in good repair.

All forms of transportation involve geographic information and, therefore, can be managed more efficiently with GIS.

Simple, but very powerful

To understand the complexities, and to stay ahead of the ceaseless rounds of repair, redesign, and new construction, transportation managers have increasingly turned to geographic information systems, or GIS.

A GIS, simply put, is a spatial database. Geographic locations are stored as sets of mathematical coordinates. Information about the locations is stored in tables that are linked to the locations.

Different spatial information is stored in different files, or layers. These layers can be viewed simultaneously, and in just about any combination. The system can also be queried to extract information from these layers. Which intersections have the most accidents, and which kinds of accidents occur most frequently? What time of day do they usually occur? These are some examples of questions a GIS database could answer.

You can also, of course, use a GIS to make maps. Maps of street networks, of train lines, of bus routes. Not just static maps, either. Because digital maps can be updated constantly, you can make maps that show the current position of a train, for example, or a snowplow, or a fire truck. You can make maps of routes that change from day to day.

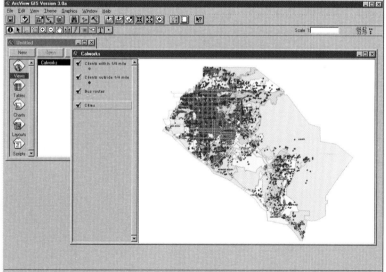

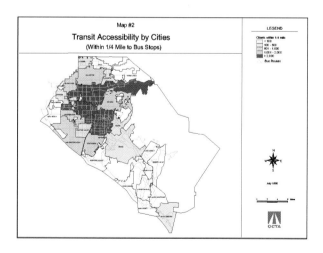

Using software like ArcView® GIS, managers in the transportation industry can monitor customers, track vehicles, and map routes. For example, Orange County Transportation Authority measures accessibility to its bus stops.

Anywhere you want to be

GIS describes a broad range of software products, from server-based technologies like ARC/INFO® to desktop solutions like ArcView GIS to Internet solutions like MapObjects® Internet Map Server. In the transportation industry, GIS is useful because it can merge data regardless of the original measuring scheme used to capture it.

This unique capability is possible because GIS systems have a linear referencing system that assigns locations to objects according to their distance to or from something else. This linear system recognizes all points along a highway or railway, not just ¹/₁₀-mile markers or intersections, for example, so the user can "query" or "view" any place along the network. In current versions of GIS software, this linear referencing capability is called dynamic segmentation (or *dyn seg* for short).

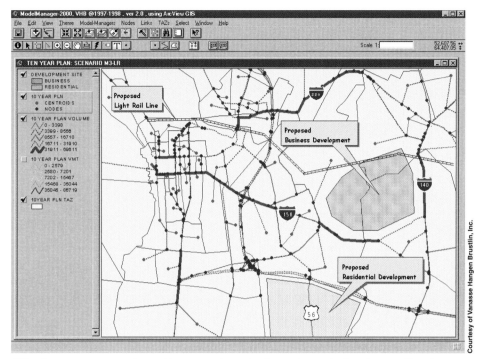

GIS software programs are also used to create and map development scenarios in order to predict where future transportation services will be required.

Courtesy of Vanasse Hangen Brustlin, Inc.

Keeping highways in good repair...

Transportation departments use GIS to design and construct highways, taking into account not only the physical realities of slope and drainage, but less tangible qualities like fragile environments and scenic beauties. Safety engineers use GIS to look for places where the same types of accidents occur so they can redesign the roads or change the signs and signals.

Highway departments maintain roads and manage their fleets of snowplows and line-painting trucks with GIS. Information about potholes, cracks, and repair schedules is maintained in the spatial database. Even complaints about the roads from drivers and reports of accidents from police departments are part of the database and thus part of the process of deciding what to repair and when to repair it.

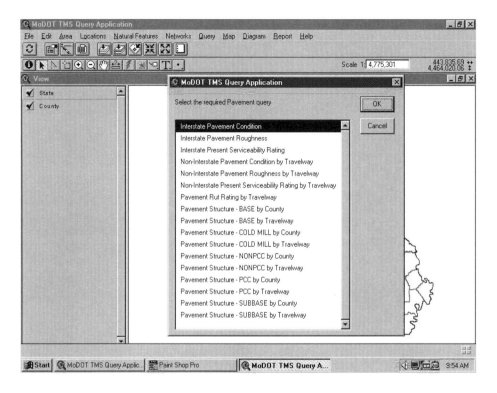

The Missouri Department of Transportation maintains a database of its entire highway system that includes a surprising amount of detail about every mile of pavement in the state.

...and traffic flowing smoothly

Urban traffic engineers use GIS to keep traffic moving smoothly and safely along the streets of their cities. Diagrams of intersections and inventories of signal control equipment are integrated into their system databases. And the locations of signals are tied to streets, accident files, and traffic count data.

GIS is used to predict future congestion and pollution, too, and to solve those problems as well. GIS gives engineers the data-based means to encourage people to reduce their dependence on new roads: to stop driving alone and ride in carpools, use public transit, ride bicycles, stagger work shifts, or even work at home. GIS helps match carpoolers by where they live and work, by the hours they work, and even by whether they prefer to ride or drive, or to smoke or not.

Recently, GIS has been incorporated into the emerging area of intelligent transportation systems (ITS), where traditional basemaps are updated in real time with information on lane closures and traffic levels, which is then provided to traffic operations, enforcement, and emergency response teams.

The ability to visualize the future is often helpful in deciding how to manage transportation issues. This graphic shows how the Southern California Association of Governments uses ArcView GIS to help decide how many new freeways to build by the year 2020.

Information-gathering tools

With GIS playing a larger role in the transportation industry, state and local governments, as well as public transit operators and shipping companies, have a wider variety of instruments and tools for collecting and processing data.

In-pavement sensors, red-light cameras, and closed-caption television (CCTV) equipment are being installed at intersections or along highways to help detect the speed and volume of traffic flow and adjust signs and signals accordingly. Global positioning systems (GPS) are being installed in taxis, trains, and even snowplows. Onboard computers can collect information from a vehicle's operating system and upload it by satellite link, along with the vehicle's position, obtained by a GPS receiver.

All of the above are examples of data that can be loaded into a geographic information system.

These images of an accident in progress are striking examples of the rich data available for use in geographic information systems. (Photos courtesy of Victoria Police Traffic Camera Office, Victoria, Australia.)

Commuter world

Railways around the world use GIS to manage real estate and facility databases to organize data for several different departments: engineering, emergency operations, and railway maintenance, among others. They use GIS to keep track of where locomotives are as they run, so any problems (detected with onboard sensors) can be repaired immediately at the nearest service facility.

Public transit agencies use GIS to plan and analyze bus routes, combining route databases with residential and business demographics to find ways to get more riders and to lower costs.

Commuter railways, subways, and light rail operators are starting to provide electronic maps to customers, at stations and over the Internet, showing train positions and arrival and departure times.

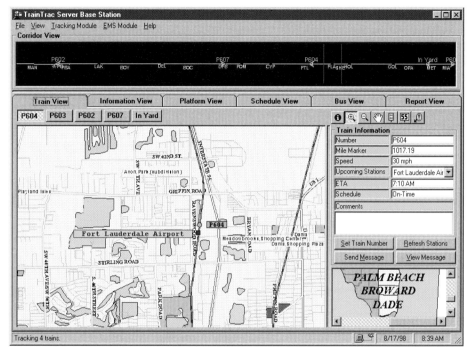

Maps like this one help the Tri-County Commuter Rail Authority provide customers with more accurate information about when a train will arrive.

Airports as good neighbors

Airport authorities use GIS to plan runways and parking lots, of course, but they also use its three-dimensional capabilities to look at flight paths and the noise contours generated by passing planes. With this information, they can plan landing and takeoff paths that stay clear of tall buildings and away from residential areas.

Airlines use these systems to analyze flight routes and plane capacities to see where they might add a route or change a destination and to plan rerouting when weather forces some airports to close.

The airline industry is using GIS more and more, not only to provide information to customers about whether a plane is on time or delayed, but also to monitor three-dimensional data like noise contours to decide how to modify landing and takeoff paths.

The road ahead

Current estimates show that approximately ten thousand transportation industry professionals use GIS to plan, design, construct, operate, and maintain roadway, rail, aviation, port, and fleet facilities around the world. As GIS becomes more commonplace in their projects, and new applications are found for the technology, its use is expected to triple in the next three to five years.

Public access via the Internet will allow spatially enabled transportation databases to be made available to a majority of citizens. Clearly, GIS is a critical tool for today's and tomorrow's transportation manager, offering as it does the opportunity to communicate more quickly and effectively with associates, policy makers, contractors, neighboring jurisdictions, and the public.

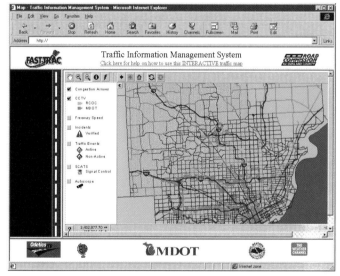
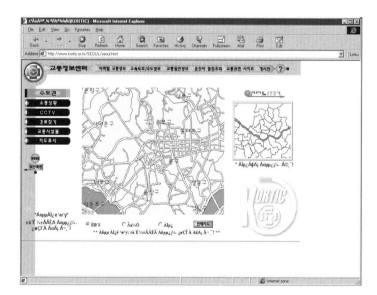

Transportation departments all over the world are using GIS software to create real-time maps and make information available to their customers via the Internet.

The case studies

The twelve case studies in this book demonstrate that GIS is capable of helping balance the needs and desires of people to travel with the contradictory but equally compelling need for clean air and uncongested roads.

Although it is impossible to address every issue of transportation management, an effort has been made to be representative. Even if your particular branch of the transportation industry isn't covered, chances are you'll recognize some common concerns, realize new solutions, and discover useful problem-solving strategies.

Chapter 2

Keeping the highways smooth and safe

The surfaces of roads and highways take a terrific pounding by the cars and trucks that travel them. The heat of summer and the ice of winter, the salt that melts the ice and the rain that washes the salt away, these all take their toll. The cracks and potholes that result have to be repaired, and sooner rather than later. If caught soon enough, damage to roads can be repaired quickly and cheaply simply by laying a fresh coat of blacktop over them, a process known as single-course overlay.

In this chapter, you'll see how New York State's Department of Transportation uses GIS to overlay data—about pavement condition, accident locations, and traffic volume—before they use blacktop to overlay the roads.

15,000 miles worth

The New York State Department of Transportation is one of the oldest and largest in the United States, managing 15,000 miles of state highways, 20,000 bridges, 4,600 miles of railroads, 600 aviation facilities, and 12 ports.

Since the 1980s, the department has kept track of all this with a growing collection of independent computer systems, each developed for a specific task.

New York State has the nation's second highest number of cars, crowded within 49,000 square miles.

Using data from different systems

Each of these unique systems used unique terminology and referencing methods to describe location. Some, like the department's pavement management system, used mile-points, distances measured from the county line. Others, like the safety management system, described location using the permanent reference markers posted along the highways every tenth of a mile.

The different measuring schemes made it difficult to use data from different systems together. But to get a complete picture of highway conditions, engineers had to have a way to do just that.

Reference markers posted along New York's state highways every tenth of a mile, like this one on Interstate 88, provided positions used for some DOT databases, while other databases were referenced by distance from the county line, calculated by distance-measuring instruments (shown below).

GIS pulls it together

Their solution was to use GIS to create one system that would allow everyone in the department to view and analyze these different kinds of data.

They first encoded the mile-point data and reference marker data to a standard digital map as separate ARC/INFO route systems. That data was then combined with attribute data residing in various program areas in Albany and eleven regional offices. Basemap data including the route systems resides on a server in Albany, and both ARC/INFO and ArcView GIS are shared over the department's wide area network.

Using ArcView GIS, data from any of the systems can be queried and overlaid for analysis, even though it's still maintained by the individual programs.

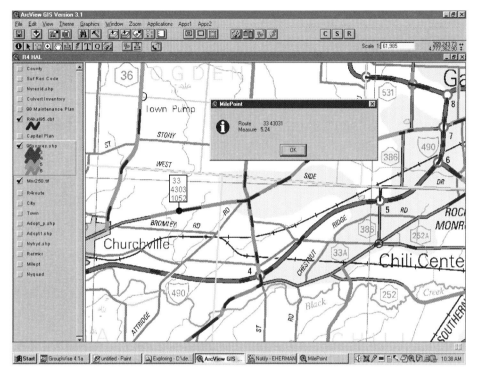

With dynamic segmentation, the department can encode the mile-point and reference marker measuring schemes to a standard digital map able to show both data types, such as this map with both pavement management data (mile-point) and safety data (reference marker).

What needs repair

Finding and viewing information about the state's highways and the projects scheduled for each typically starts with selecting a study area on the state map by circling it or by typing in a county name, another political boundary, or a project identification number.

On this map, the manager queries the system for projects in three hamlets, and color codes them by status (ongoing or planned) and by type (subsurface repair or single-course overlay). With information attached to these projects, like schedules and funding, the manager could produce a range of reports and maps of area projects and their dollar values for an elected official, or oversized maps for public meetings to explain when local projects will take place, how long they'll take, how much they'll cost, and where detours will be.

The GIS is also used to answer inquiries from the public and media. With the aid of ArcView GIS, the staff can locate projects quickly and view attached documents like funding breakdowns and schedules. They look at all the projects in certain areas or happening at certain times, such as within the next twelve months.

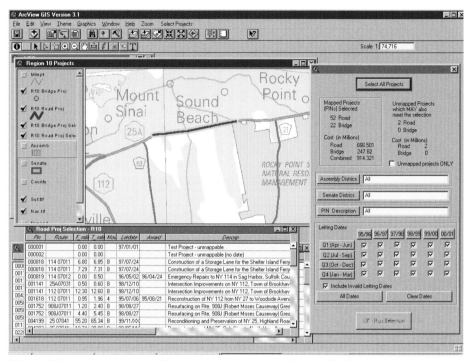

With the "Commissioner's Interface," managers can view projects by assembly districts or letting dates.

Rating the projects

To determine where money will be spent, managers in the capital program use the GIS to evaluate a project's benefit to the public and its importance in relation to other projects.

Departmental goals, like improving safety and reducing congestion, can be measured project by project using the GIS.

Using ArcView GIS, managers retrieve pavement condition scores for areas being evaluated and assign colors to indicate poor (priority) and fair (nonpriority). They then query the system for safety scores and congestion scores, and rate them, too.

These three themes are overlaid on the map. In one area, the segments that intersect are all rated poor, so the managers allocate money to this one right away.

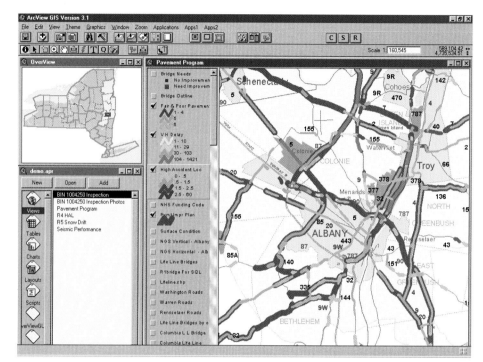

From this map, a manager can tell where capital improvement projects will help the DOT meet several of its goals, such as the corridor just west of Albany.

Rating the road segments

With the funding allocated to make repairs, regional maintenance engineers are able to schedule individual improvement projects. Their first task is determining which highway segments need minimal treatment (a single-course overlay), and which need either more work or no work at all.

The engineers request pavement condition scores from Albany. These scores are updated yearly by visual inspections and range from 1 to 10, with 10 being excellent. Segments scoring 7 or higher don't need an overlay and are dropped from the map. Segments scoring 5 or less definitely need an overlay but may need other work as well. They are set aside for individual study.

Only those segments scoring 6, as shown on this map, are candidates for single-course overlay.

Once the candidate segments for single-course overlay are identified, the department can schedule them for improvement.

Scheduling the projects

Because the single-course overlay projects are scattered around the district, the engineers need to decide which order they'll be done in. In the past, they decided by how important they thought the highway was to commuters and by whether alternative routes were available to handle the diverted traffic.

With the GIS, that became both easier and more accurate. The engineers overlay traffic volume data, congestion data, and transit routes for each segment that's a candidate for a single-course overlay. They then rank the projects and assign a project identification number to each to indicate when the repaving will begin.

This project identification number is stored in the capital program information system so other departments, and management, can access it when making queries about the project. The project ID numbers are also used by employees in the department's residencies (smaller offices that support local road-improvement projects) to view a project's location and to print maps for road work crews.

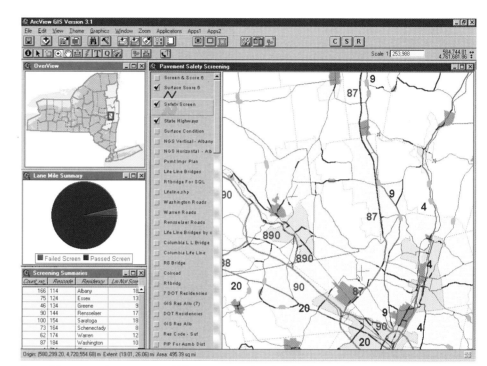

From this map, engineers can see which segments can be scheduled for single-course overlay right away, and (in green) where a safety analysis should be performed first.

Accident statistics

With the single-course overlays scheduled, the engineers now use the GIS to
view roads with scores of 5 or lower, those
that need more work before they can be
repaved.

The engineers first query the safety management system for accident data. In this
case, they are most concerned about
single-car accidents, where a car runs off
the road or hits a fixed object. From this
list, another query isolates the segments
with many single-car accidents, 40 percent
or more. Using ARC/INFO software's
Event Transform and Event Overlay com-
mands to combine the ArcView GIS event
theme with the pavement scores shows
which segments have had the most accidents. They use data in the subsystems to
find out why.

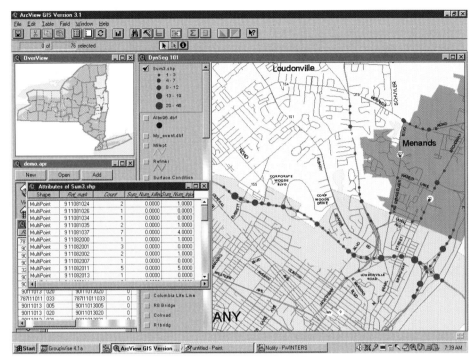

*By viewing accident locations and summarizing them for display by type and severity, managers can make
decisions about how to improve safety, such as adding warning signs or flashing lights.*

Flashing lights

Each incident can be displayed as a point. By clicking on an accident point, the engineer retrieves its attribute data, including the officer's accident report, which often provides useful information, such as the motorist saying he or she didn't see a merge sign and ran off the road when the lane ended.

By viewing data from the accident reports, the engineer sees a pattern develop. During peak traffic hours, the majority of accidents at this location happen when cars fail to merge and so drive onto the shoulder. The engineer uses ArcView GIS to create a report that includes a map of the lanes and the signs, and a map of accident locations, and recommends that flashing lights be installed along the road to warn of the lane ending. After the flashing signal has been installed, the segment will be scheduled for a single-course overlay and the pavement surface repainted.

The highlighted point shows statistics for an accident that occurred on March 12, 1996, in which one person was injured.

Hardware

Sun™ workstation servers in each regional office with Windows 95® PCs connected with a LAN. A WAN T1 connection connects regional offices to Albany (residencies dial in).

Software

ARC/INFO (data creation and basemap maintenance)

ArcView GIS (end user applications)

ArcPress™

ArcView Spatial Analyst

CAD Reader

Data

24,000-scale raster data

24,000-scale vector data (roads, boundaries, hydrology, and utilities)

250,000-scale statewide data on roads, boundaries, hydrography, and utilities, generalized from 24,000-scale data

Soils data (borings)

Demographic/Census data

Traffic data

Safety data

Pavement condition data

Bridges data

Environmental data (e.g., wetlands, historical sites)

Acknowledgments

Thanks to William F. Johnson, head of the Mapping and GIS Section, and to Frank Winters, GIS Manager, of the New York State Department of Transportation.

New York State

Department of Transportation

Chapter 3

No new freeways

Within twenty years, southern California, with some of the most congested freeways in the United States, will have six million more people. Yet not a single new freeway will be built. The plan is to more effectively use existing roadways, to improve freeways with toll and carpool lanes, and to encourage mass transit alternatives like rail, shuttles, and buses. To be effective, each change must be considered at a regional level, so traffic snarls aren't just moved from one town to another.

In this chapter, you'll see how the Southern California Association of Governments (SCAG) uses GIS to study the region's transportation issues and make recommendations to the agencies that manage transportation assets.

Y2K, plus 20

SCAG is a regional planning agency comprised of 184 cities in Ventura, Los Angeles, Orange, San Bernardino, Riverside, and Imperial counties. This region has more than sixteen million people and some of the country's most congested roadways and polluted air.

By 2020, six million more people will likely live here, further congesting the region's freeways and arterial roads. Long-distance commuters and widely distributed businesses mean many more cars will crowd onto the roads. As commute times lengthen, workers, employers, and visitors become more frustrated. Such high levels of congestion could make businesses relocate and scare off tourists.

To prevent that from happening, SCAG and its member agencies use GIS to see which roads get congested, and when,

and to identify the best ways to reduce congestion on those roads, such as van-pools, carpools, or staggered work hours.

More people and more cars are clogging southern California's freeways. SCAG member agencies use GIS to view congestion levels and plan transit alternatives to keep the region livable.

The SCAG decongestant

A typical project in the planning department at SCAG's Los Angeles headquarters looks at congestion around employers in projected high-growth industries, like biotechnology companies. The planner wants to head off problems at these sites by suggesting mass transit alternatives to these companies.

The planner starts with a digital map of southern California and defines the study area by circling it or entering a geographic name like a county or city into ArcView GIS. After selecting from a list of industries to view the locations of biotechnology companies and the number of their employees, the planner adds traffic volume data to the map, both current and that projected for twenty years. Projected volumes are calculated by SCAG's regional transportation model, which is continuously updated with actual traffic count information recorded by sensors embedded in the roadways.

On this map, red indicates heavy congestion, where trip times will increase by 70 to 100 percent, and orange indicates where trip times will increase by 50 to 70 percent. Because no rail or bus service is available near the work site, the planner will approach these companies about starting vanpools or carpools, or staggering work hours.

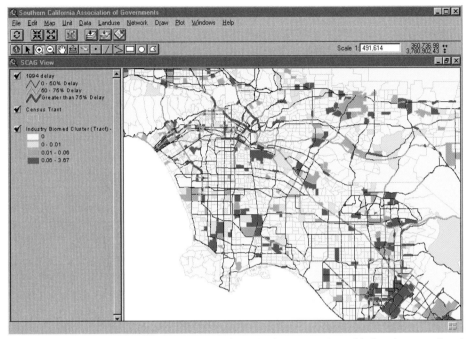

From this map, the planner can see concentrations of biotechnology companies and look at the congestion of surrounding freeways, which employees and suppliers will travel.

A reasonable alternative

Another SCAG planner is looking at traffic volumes in Orange County and whether building a fixed-rail line in a busy commuting corridor would reduce traffic.

The planner starts with census data to create a map showing where people live and where they work, then adds traffic congestion data. The dark blue areas, where commuters spend the longest times in traffic, coincide with the corridor being proposed for the rail line.

So far, so good. However, since studies indicate that fixed-rail is mainly used by commuters when stations are within walking distance (a quarter mile) of their home and office, the planner uses the GIS to count how many people live and work that close to the line. From this, the planner realizes there are too few riders to justify the cost of building and operating the fixed-rail line.

The planner then views businesses within 5 miles of the corridor and selects the five largest to target with information about vanpools and smart shuttles, two transit alternatives that should work well in this area.

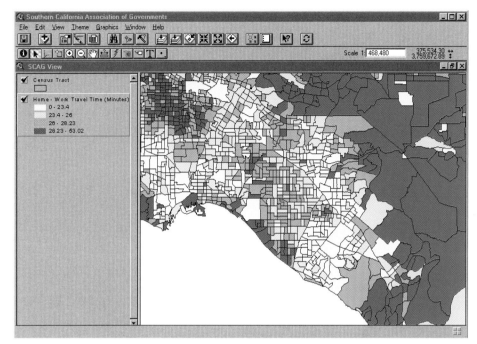

By overlaying census data and time (in minutes) spent commuting, planners can estimate the success of transit alternatives like rail lines or smart shuttles.

Getting the carless to work

In addition to supplying employers with information about alternatives to "one car, one person" commuting, SCAG uses GIS to identify people who would benefit from ride-sharing and vanpool programs, such as former welfare recipients searching for work.

A planner uses occupational data from the state employment department to determine which businesses in Orange County are hiring low-skilled workers and where they are located. These are shown on a map, along with the locations of the county's job-training centers.

Next, census tracts where current welfare recipients live are added along with highways and bus routes.

Because many of these people do not have a car, the planner wants to see if they live and work within a quarter mile of a bus stop. Creating a quarter-mile buffer around the stops and summarizing the results in a table shows that many people living in Orange County could use the bus to get to these employment and training sites.

The planner creates a list of the companies near the bus stops to contact with route information and a list of those outside the buffer to target with vanpool and carpool program information.

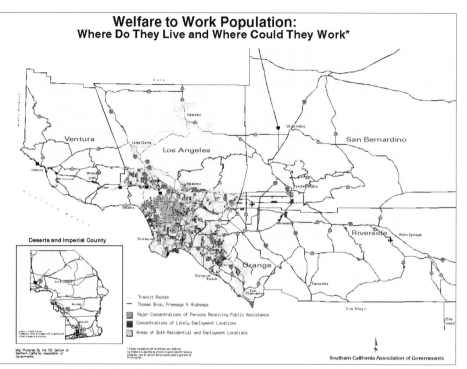

Maps are created to show where former welfare recipients live, where they might work, and the available transit alternatives since they are unlikely to own automobiles.

Crossing the boundaries

In addition to using GIS in-house, SCAG has distributed ACCESS, a GIS application built with ArcView GIS, to member agencies. With ACCESS, local planners can view portions of SCAG's traffic, business, and demographic data for their own projects. With ACCESS, the region's planners are able to share information and come up with solutions that reach beyond political borders.

A transportation planner in Santa Ana uses the system to view SCAG's projected traffic volumes for Interstate 5, which runs alongside the city. From the opening screen, the planner clicks on Santa Ana and then uses the 2020 button to add traffic volumes forecast for that year. From the map, the planner sees which sections of I-5 (in red) will be the most congested.

The planner zooms to the street network to see where frustrated drivers might exit the freeway. Because significant congestion is also projected for this arterial road, the planner views a table about the road to see if it could be widened to accommodate the overflow. Since this road runs into the next city, where it would narrow again and slow traffic, the planner uses the GIS data and maps in ACCESS to discuss the road-widening project. Changes made to the road will be reported to SCAG to input into the traffic-forecasting model.

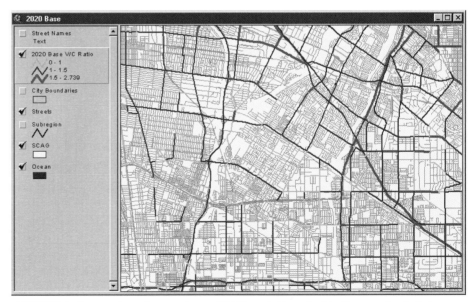

ACCESS lets planners at member agencies use SCAG's projections about traffic congestion in their own studies and coordinate projects across political boundaries.

Keeping the plan up to date

As local agencies improve roads, they send updates to SCAG on hard-copy maps for incorporation into the Regional Transportation Plan, a document required by a number of state and federal mandates that outlines the goals, objectives, and policies for the SCAG region.

This document, which can be viewed at www.scag.ca.gov, gives local planners an overview of changes proposed for the region's road, rail, and bus networks, and how these changes would affect future traffic volumes.

Local transportation planners use these forecasts to make adjustments in their arterial road network, proposing rail stations, bus stops, or smart shuttle collection points.

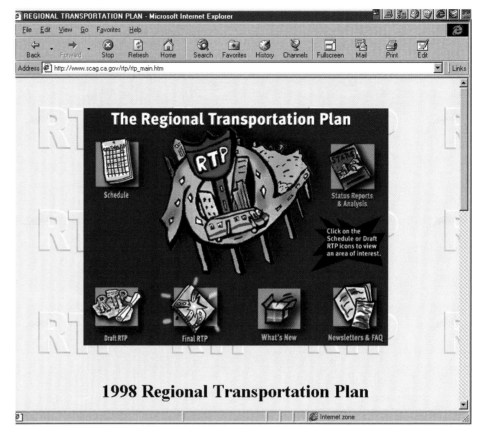

Anyone connected to the Internet can download the Regional Transportation Plan in either HTML or PDF format.

From transportation highway to information highway

In the future, SCAG will make some of its GIS data and applications available over the Internet to transportation planning agencies, economic development agencies, university planning and geography departments, and environmental planning agencies. These agencies and institutions, also hard at work on solving gridlock and making the area more livable, would use the SCAG data in their own research projects and provide feedback and ideas to the agency.

Unclogging southern California's roads won't be easy, but without a cooperative effort like ACCESS it would be impossible.

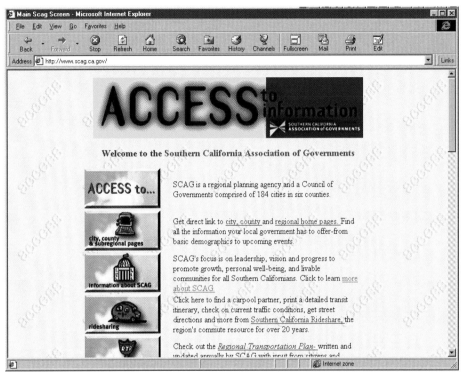

In the future, other agencies involved in fighting gridlock will be able to access SCAG data on the Internet.

Hardware

PC workstations supporting GIS and
Internet applications

Software

ARC/INFO

ArcView GIS

MapObjects

TRANPLAN (Urban Analysis Group)

Microsoft® Windows NT®

Data

U.S. Bureau of the Census

1990 Census Transportation Planning
Package (CTPP)

SCAG regional data

Acknowledgments

Thanks to Terry Bills of the Southern
California Association of Governments.

Chapter 4

Unlocking gridlock

Gridlock used to be a term limited to describing midday traffic in Manhattan or the morning and evening commutes in southern California. No more. Almost any road anywhere now is crowded with too many people, often only one person per car.

So state and local governments are encouraging people to ride together or even leave their cars at home and ride their bicycles or walk to work. In Washington State, the Commute Trip Reduction Law, passed in 1991 as part of the state's Clean Air Act, requires local jurisdictions to encourage employers with a workforce of one hundred or more to reduce the amount of driving their employees do.

In this chapter, you'll see how Spokane County, with ninety major employers, is using GIS to find which employees could walk or ride bikes to work, and to link up the ones who can carpool.

Keep the car in the garage

Spokane County is one of four Washington counties bordering Idaho. During the past twenty-five years, the county's population has increased from 275,000 to 409,000, with most growth in unincorporated areas north and east of the city of Spokane.

In 1991, the state passed a law that requires employers with one hundred or more full-time day employees to reduce the driving their employees do by encouraging them to carpool, vanpool, ride the bus, walk, or bicycle to work. Some people can even work from home or compress their work schedules.

Commuters compete for space on a congested Spokane arterial.

The TransMatch solution

At the time, Spokane's local transit agency offered a free manual ride-matching service but its data was often dated—people had often either already found ride-matching partners or had moved from the area.

In 1993, Spokane County offered to help develop a computerized ride-matching service. The initial system, called TransMatch, was written by the county's system services department using FoxPro® version 1.0. It matched commuters by origin and destination.

The following year, the county improved TransMatch by incorporating ArcView GIS version 2.0, Microsoft Access, Wessex (GDT) street data, and Spokane County's street network data.

The street network data, maintained by the county in ARC/INFO, covers all of Spokane County. The Wessex street data covers streets in the counties surrounding Spokane and in northern Idaho for matching commuters from rural areas.

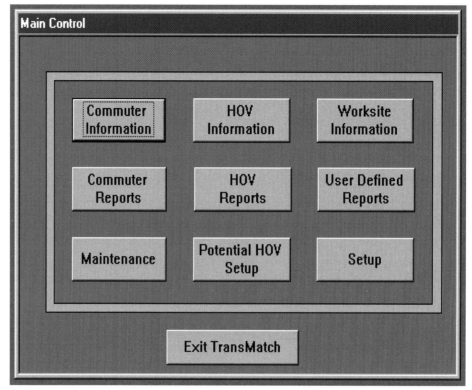

From this opening screen, the TransMatch operator can choose to enter new commuters, search for matches, or create reports.

The search begins

The county uses TransMatch to provide free ride-matching services. About one hundred work sites employing 145,000 people, or about 25 percent of the county's total workforce, have access to the service.

Those interested in the ride-matching service complete a form with their addresses (home and work), work schedule, and personal preferences, such as smoking or nonsmoking, or whether they like to drive or to ride.

Using TransMatch, the analyst clicks on Commuter Information and enters a street address for the origin and for the destination, along with the rest of the information, to search a Microsoft Access database of about twelve hundred applicants.

The default search radius around an origin is 3,000 meters (about 2 miles) and 2,000 meters around the destination. After viewing attribute information for any matches, the analyst can select or delete candidates. If there are no matches, the analyst widens TransMatch's search radius to 5 miles, and then 10.

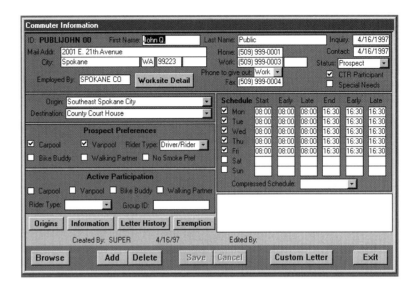

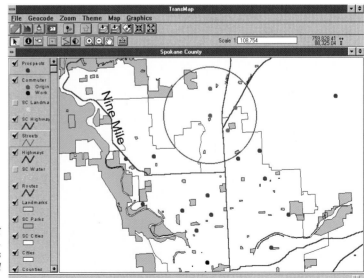

Data from the ride-matching forms is entered into the system. Then analysts search for matches within a defined radius to find potential ride-sharing partners.

The search ends

If no match is found within the radii, the analyst uses TransMatch's corridor-matching capability, written to match people farther from one another, but who commute along the same highways and arterials.

The analyst uses Route Match to identify any people living close to the applicant's route. Another tool, Corridor Match, searches for people living along the commute corridor who could meet the applicant at a park-and-ride facility.

Using the GIS to see potential matches also allows the analyst to see any barriers to the commuting arrangement such as rivers or mountains, which appear as color-coded landmarks on the map. The analyst can zoom in to the barrier and see how it will affect the potential match.

When matches are found, a letter is sent to the applicant with the names and telephone numbers of potential rideshare partners.

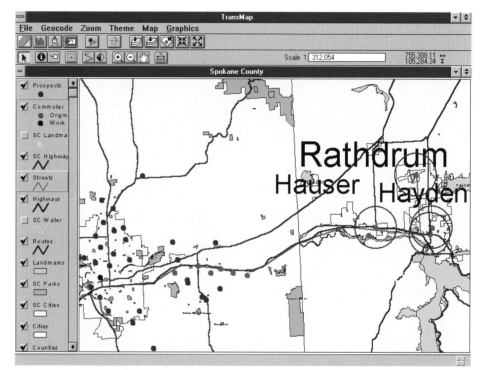

Corridor searching matches people who may live many miles apart but travel along the same highway, as shown on this map, with northern Idaho on the right and Washington State (Spokane) on the left.

Keeping tabs on the system

TransMatch can also be used to generate reports about the status of an agency's ride-matching services. These can show system managers how many commuters have been matched by work site, by mode of transportation, or along corridors.

Reports can be created for employers showing how many employees from a company have received ridematch lists. The analyst enters the employer's address or name to identify the right records and sorts the participating employees into those who have been provided with matches and those who have not. The employer could use this list to follow up with applicants to see how well the carpool match worked, or if employees are still driving to work alone.

Reports can be printed to show commuters by destination or origin, or as prospective and active (matched to a carpool partner). The system also helps keep information about the commuters current. Four weeks after an application is received, the applicant gets a letter from the county requesting confirmation that they're still interested in the ride-matching service. At six months, they receive a letter asking them to update their information. After a year, they receive a letter requesting a response if they're still looking for a ride-sharing partner. If no response is received, the applicant's name and data are deleted.

A variety of reports provide valuable information for system managers and employers. Information in TransMatch is updated by sending form letters at defined intervals to find out if the person still needs the ride-matching service.

Finding more riders

Employers in Spokane County can also get "Employee Home Locator Maps" from the county's Commute Reduction Office, a section of the Division of Engineering and Roads. These maps are created in ARC/INFO using data from the companies about where employees live and what time they need to travel to and from work.

This data is usually received as an electronic spreadsheet and ARC/INFO is used to match addresses to points on a map. Because Spokane County is one of a few regions in the United States where residents put the street direction before an address, the GIS analyst has to change the data before it can be used, "North 815 Jefferson" to "815 N. Jefferson," for instance. The data is then imported into ARC/INFO and geocoded to the county's GIS road layer. The dots on the map are numbered to correspond to the employees and can be color coded to display additional information, such as whether they work days or nights.

The entire process takes about an hour per map.

Once completed, the map is given to the work site's transportation coordinator, who uses the information to match interested employees with car and vanpools.

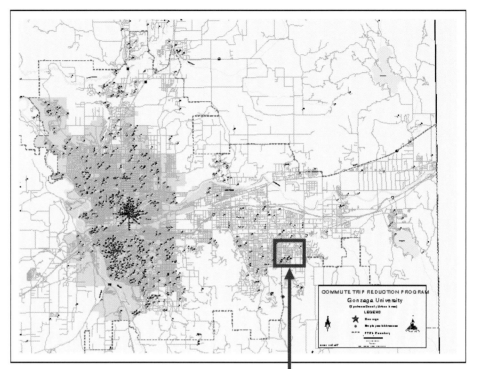

Employers in Spokane County use GIS to find employees who live close to each other and who work the same shifts to set up carpools and vanpools.

And even more riders

Since 1993, when Spokane County passed a local ordinance to reduce drive-alone commutes, participating employers have seen solo commuting drop by 13 percent and miles traveled fall by 10.2 percent. Carpooling accounts for roughly 16 percent of all travel to work sites in the Commute Trip Reduction program.

Spokane Transit recently joined Spokane County as a TransMatch partner. With TransMatch being promoted to the general public, it's expected to draw more applicants so even more people can be matched with car and vanpools.

Car and vanpooling is on the rise in Spokane, thanks, in part, to TransMatch.

Hardware

PC and Sun workstations

Software

ArcView GIS
ARC/INFO
Microsoft Access

Data

Spokane County and Wessex street data

Acknowledgments

Thanks to Melanie Rose, Transportation Demand Management Manager of the Spokane County Commute Trip Reduction Office, and to Ian Von Essen, GIS Network Manager of Spokane County.

Chapter 5

When it's the roads that aren't safe

Traffic collisions happen for many reasons, but when they start to occur frequently and at the same location, transportation engineers start to suspect causes other than careless drivers—narrow roads, tight corners, intersections with no turn lanes, traffic lights that go from red to green before the intersection clears.

The City of San Leandro, in northern California, uses GIS to examine areas where traffic collisions have occurred and decide what to fix and which things to fix first.

San Leandro at the crossroads

San Leandro is a city at the crossroads. North along I-880 lies the city of Oakland, with busy air and seaports. To the south is Silicon Valley. To the east along I-238 and 580 is the agricultural San Joaquin Valley.

The highways connecting these regions are heavily traveled. Trucks with loads from Oakland's air and seaports jostle with commuters. In and around San Leandro is 50 million square feet of industrial and warehouse space that trucking companies use for storage or as a base of operations.

Photo courtesy of J. R. Accettola, Napa, California.

Accidents like this one can sometimes be prevented when roadways are modified in ways that make them safer for everyone.

The congestion equation

When highways become clogged and travelers and trucks move onto surface streets, local congestion worsens and more accidents occur.

To find out where collisions were happening and why, traffic engineers used to rely on collision reports. Filed by location of the accident (e.g., East 14th and Davis Street, or midblock between San Leandro Boulevard and Alvarado Street), these took time and perseverance to locate.

In 1998, the Transportation Division contracted with Crossroads Software, a GIS software developer in Brea, California, that specializes in traffic collision systems, to create a system using ArcView GIS that engineers could use to find accidents by location, cause, date, time of day, or type of vehicle.

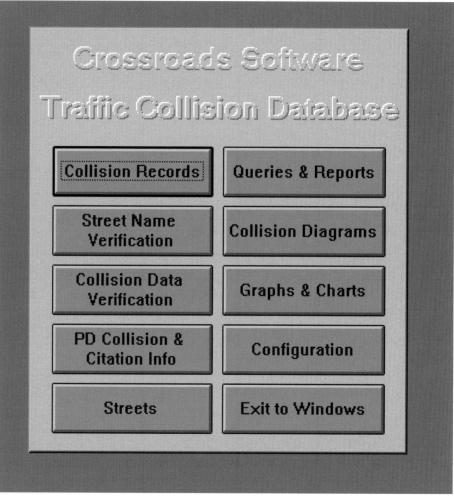

A specialized database like this one, created by Crossroads Software, makes the search for information faster and more efficient.

How safe are our streets?

The division's transportation engineers use the system to research complaints about the safety of streets or intersections.

From the opening screen, an engineer types in an address or place name, and ArcView GIS zooms to the location. The GIS database includes aerial photographs, so the engineers can see what the intersections look like, too.

Overlaying additional data will show all of the collisions that have occurred on a specific street during the past year, each collision categorized by cause, the type of vehicle involved, the time of day, or severity (property damage only, injuries, or fatality).

Aerial photographs of intersections may help engineers see why certain ones seem to be a problem.

Broadsides on Davis Street

Several complaints have been received about the increasingly heavy traffic on Davis Street, which runs east–west through the city. Even though this is a state highway, the city is responsible for detecting problems and working with the California Department of Transportation (Caltrans) to resolve them.

An engineer enters the street name to view it, overlays aerial photography, and queries the historical database for collisions along this road during the past three years. Other queries begin to reveal what has been causing the collisions. A summary of collisions by time of day, for instance, shows that many happen during the afternoon and early evening. Another summary might show more fender-benders during rainy days.

Querying the system on the type of collision shows that most collisions on Davis Street are broadsides. The engineer concludes that the traffic signals along Davis Street aren't giving people enough time to clear the intersection. He suggests keeping the yellow light on longer so traffic can clear.

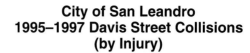

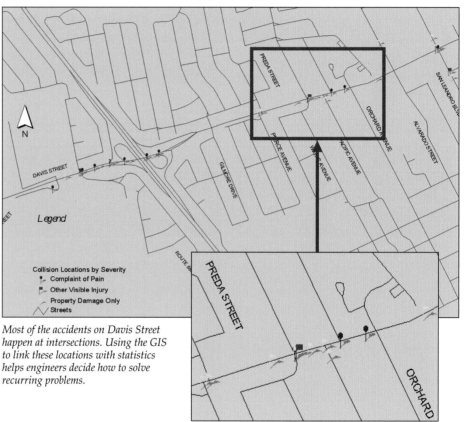

Most of the accidents on Davis Street happen at intersections. Using the GIS to link these locations with statistics helps engineers decide how to solve recurring problems.

The left-turn dilemma

The map also shows clusters of left-turn collisions at several intersections. Visits to the sites will show if the streets need separate left-turn lanes, raised median islands, or left-turn signals.

After a visit, the engineer will present the findings to Caltrans and to other departments to help them decide how to spend city or state monies to fix the problems.

Being able to spot clusters of accident locations helps determine which intersections should be improved first.

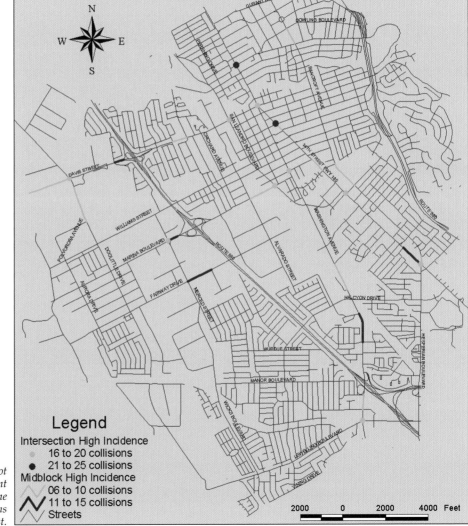

City of San Leandro
Top 10 Intersection and Midblock Collision Locations

Legend

Intersection High Incidence
- 16 to 20 collisions
- 21 to 25 collisions

Midblock High Incidence
- 06 to 10 collisions
- 11 to 15 collisions
- Streets

2000   0   2000   4000 Feet

A turn too far

San Leandro is an old city, with still a fair number of old and narrow intersections, intersections difficult to negotiate by the big trucks that drive its streets.

Looking at a map of truck accidents over the past two years, an engineer notices a prominent cluster around one intersection. The ArcView GIS table connected to this map shows that all these accidents have involved trucks hitting the traffic signal standards, one of them several times a year.

Because this intersection is part of an important delivery route, the engineer recommends widening the intersection and setting signal standards back from the street to accommodate the trucks.

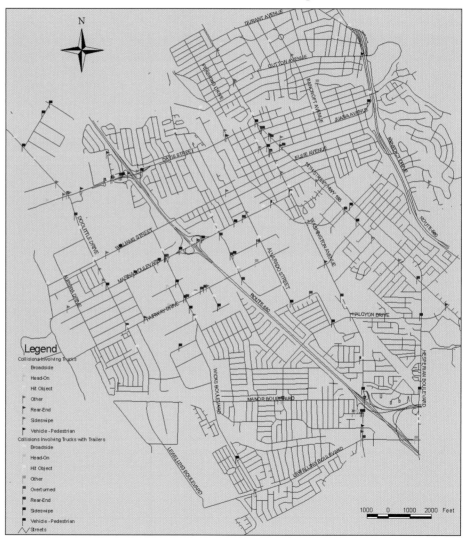

**City of San Leandro
1996–1997 Collisions Involving Trucks**

Accident locations along important delivery routes will be modified first.

Police records—the final frontier

The city is improving its traffic collision system in 1999 by linking police records with another Crossroads module, which links other documents to the collision database. This will make the collision data collected after an accident available through ArcView GIS. This data, especially the sketches made by police, is valuable in understanding why collisions happened and how they can be prevented.

Linking police sketches and records to other data in the GIS can help determine why accidents happen and how they can be prevented.

Hardware

Dell PC running Windows NT

Software

ArcView GIS version 3.1

Data

Historical collision records going back five years

City-street GIS network (maintained with ARC/INFO in the Engineering Division)

Aerial photography

Facilities data

Traffic volume data

Acknowledgments

Thanks to Raymond E. Davis III, P.E., P.T.O.E., Transportation Administrator, City of San Leandro.

Chapter 6

Filling the buses

Bus stops are a familiar part of the landscape, even in car-glutted southern California. So familiar, we probably don't give much thought to where they're located, unless of course we ride the buses or run the bus companies. If we ride buses, we don't want to have to walk more than a couple of blocks to the nearest stop. And if we operate the bus company, we don't want our clients to have to walk very far to use our services.

In this chapter, you'll see how the Orange County Transportation Authority (OCTA) in southern California uses GIS to find out all they can about bus stops—who lives near them, what businesses are located there, and what other attractions like parks or civic centers are nearby—and decide where to spend money on improvements and where to extend service hours.

Fifty-three million a year

OCTA, Orange County's primary public-transit operator, operating with a yearly budget of $541 million and providing fifty-three million rides per year with local and express bus services, follows seventy-one fixed routes on Orange County's major arterial streets. The express buses run on the freeways, stopping at park-and-ride locations and at large employers like McDonnell Douglas and Disneyland.

The agency's Transportation Analysis Department has used ARC/INFO software since the early nineties to plan bus routes and decide where to put the stops. Since 1996, they have also used ArcView GIS to view and analyze data.

OCTA studies find passengers are most likely to ride buses when stops are within a quarter-mile walking distance of both their start and destination locations.

Lower the curb

Bus stops must be close to where the people who use them live and work and shop. Because many of these people are disabled, the bus stops must have curbs low enough for wheelchairs to negotiate, according to guidelines of the Americans with Disabilities Act of 1990.

In 1995, OCTA commissioned a study to see how many of its 5,941 stops had curbs low enough for wheelchairs. Only 593 did, leaving 4,348 bus stops that did not— more than 4,000 stops, OCTA realized, that weren't allowing potential customers access to their service.

With only enough funds to improve three to four hundred stops a year, the most obvious place to start was with the stops used by the most people, especially disabled people. Using GIS, the agency identified which of those stops had already been funded, and which did not need any improvements. They also assigned each stop a score for each of several categories. The higher the score, the sooner that stop would be improved.

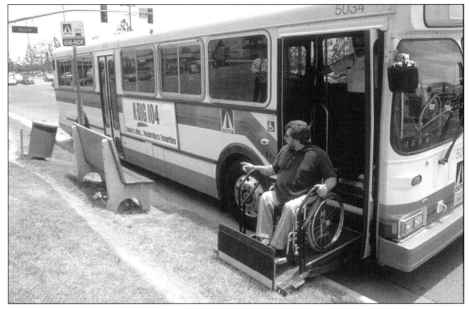

With GIS, OCTA could decide which stops to improve according to how many jobs and homes were nearby and which stops were used by disabled passengers.

Walking distance from homes and jobs

To evaluate how well their stops were serving the public, OCTA used demographic data about population and employment to find out how many people lived and worked (and shopped) within walking distance of each stop. (Walking distance was defined as ¼ mile.)

The more people living within walking distance of a stop, the more use it could be expected to get. Similarly, stops within walking distance of businesses and stores were expected to get more use than those that aren't.

So, the analysts used ArcView Network Analyst and a street centerline file to measure walking distance along the streets around each stop and counted the number of people living and working around each. Stops received one point for each person and one for each job.

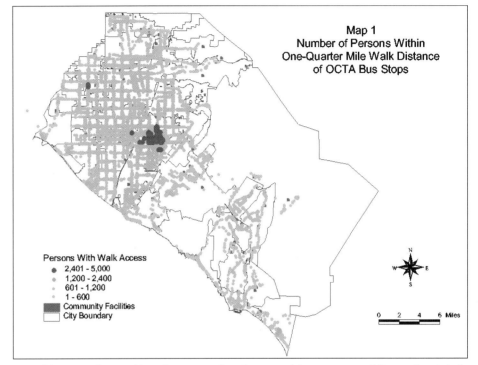

From this map, analysts could see that, compared to other areas of the county, central Orange County had higher concentrations of people living within walking distance of bus stops.

The scoring begins

Armed with these numbers, OCTA began assigning scores to stops for various qualities: accessibility, closeness to hospitals, and whether they had already received funding. The number each stop had been given, according to the number of people and jobs around it, would be multiplied by these scores. These weighted scores would be used to decide which stops to improve first. The higher the final score, the sooner the stop would be attended to.

Stops not already funded were placed into one of three categories, fully accessible (1,593 stops), partially accessible (3,652 stops), or inaccessible (696 stops).

The stops were then placed on a map created with ARC/INFO, from which analysts could see that stops in all three categories were distributed all over the county.

Fully accessible stops were given a score of zero and dropped from the study. Partially accessible and inaccessible stops got a score of 1.

Through passenger surveys, analysts found that 2,320 stops were being used by disabled people. These stops were given a score of 3.

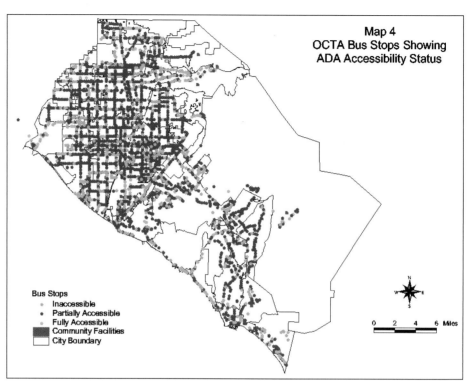

Fully accessible stops were dropped from consideration for funding.

Walking distance from hospitals and stores

Next, the analysts wanted to find which stops were close to facilities like hospitals, senior centers, and shopping centers.

These stops would need to provide access for the disabled sooner than others, so the 1,113 stops within walking distance of hospitals and other important activity centers were given a score of 3. Stops farther away were given a 2.

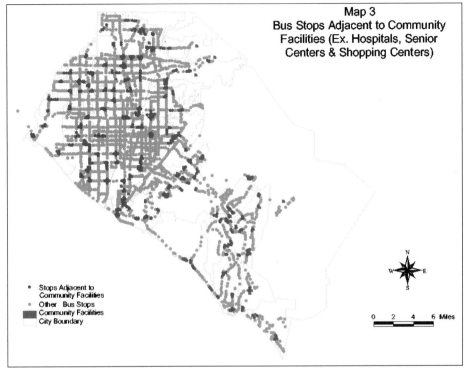

Map 3
Bus Stops Adjacent to Community
Facilities (Ex. Hospitals, Senior
Centers & Shopping Centers)

• Stops Adjacent to
   Community Facilities
• Other Bus Stops
▪ Community Facilities
   City Boundary

0   2   4   6 Miles

So that ADA improvements would be made to stops near community facilities like senior centers, OCTA gave them higher scores than stops farther away.

The improvements begin

Because they were either fully accessible or already funded, 2,747 stops scored zero. The 3,194 stops that scored higher than zero were ranked according to how soon they needed to be improved.

This data was provided to OCTA's transit staff and ADA project manager for use with ArcView GIS in explaining funding criteria and decisions to the communities waiting for their bus stops to be improved.

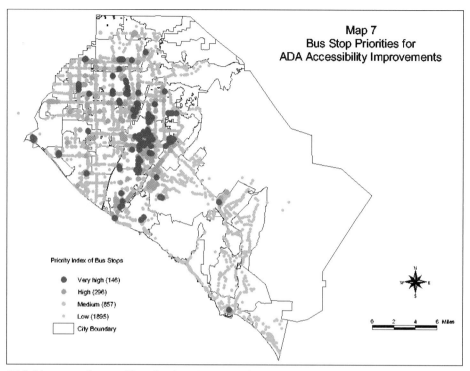

With this map, analysts could see that the priority stops for ADA improvements are in the central and northern parts of the county.

The time element

While all the scoring and ranking were going on, OCTA was examining how its schedules were serving people. So what if the stop is only 100 yards away with a nice low curb if there's no bus running?

So OCTA analysts used the GIS to overlay the number of buses and locations of workplaces for three typical work shifts—weekdays 6 A.M. to 7 P.M., weekday evenings after 7 P.M., and weekends.

Those maps showed fewer buses were available to workers in the evening and on weekends. They would have a long wait in some cases or not be able to use the buses at all to travel to and from work. OCTA used these maps to extend service hours during the week and add more buses on the weekends.

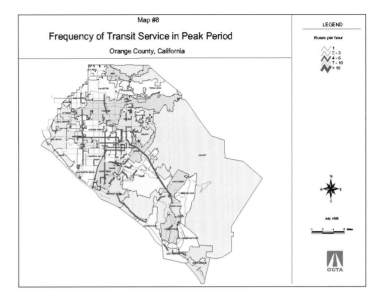

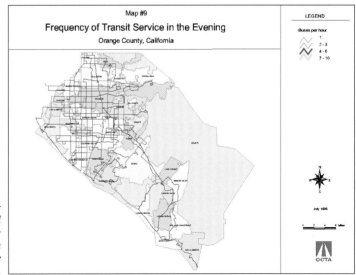

These maps show the number of buses operating on major arterial streets during mornings and evenings, Monday through Friday. During evenings and on weekends, fewer buses run on these routes, posing a transit problem for people who work those shifts.

All aboard

OCTA's Transportation Analysis Department is currently helping to design corporate databases so staff in other departments can use ArcView GIS to find, edit, view, and analyze all kinds of information.

They expect this will increase the efficiency of the departments, many of which now collect and maintain their own data, and increase ridership as routes and stops are redesigned to better serve the people and businesses in the area.

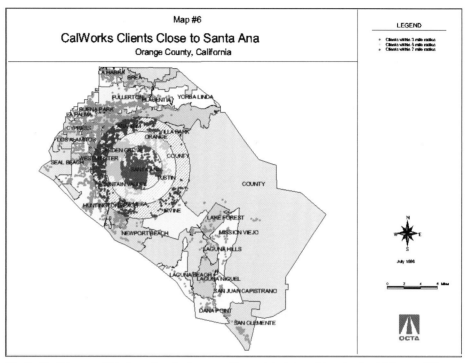

Studies like this one, which shows how far former welfare recipients travel to entry-level jobs, use GIS to combine and analyze data from several OCTA departments and state agencies like CalWorks.

Hardware

IBM® AIX® workstations, migrating in 1999 to Windows NT workstations with an HP® 9000 server

Software

ARC/INFO

ArcView GIS

ArcView Network Analyst extension

Data

OCTA ridership, route, and bus stop location data

Demographics (U.S. Bureau of the Census)

GIS street file network (Thomas Bros. Maps)

Business data (various sources, including U.S. Bureau of the Census)

Welfare recipients (Orange County Social Service Agency)

Job data (Orange County Private Industry Council)

Acknowledgments

Thanks to Shirley Hsiao, a senior transportation planner with the Orange County Transportation Authority in Orange, California.

Chapter 7

Crowded skies

Two signs of a growing city are its skyline, dominated by taller and taller buildings, and its bustling air traffic, with more and more planes ferrying people to and from all over the world. Unfortunately, the tall buildings can intrude into the airspace needed by planes. And the noise from the planes intrudes into every space.

In this chapter, you'll see how planners at the Minneapolis–St. Paul International Airport, the twelfth busiest airport in the United States, use GIS to view flight paths in three dimensions to see where objects are that planes might hit, and how they use three-dimensional GIS to monitor noise levels produced by passing planes.

More runways

The Minneapolis–St. Paul International Airport, owned and operated by the Metropolitan Airports Commission (MAC), serves more than thirty million travelers annually. By 2020 that number will increase by about 25 percent, requiring the airport to build more terminals, runways, and parking areas.

Airport planners are using GIS to analyze new runways and other structures being planned, to see where the planes will need to fly, where radar beams need to work, and how nearby buildings might interfere with flight paths.

To accommodate more passengers, the Minneapolis–St. Paul International Airport is working to improve its runways, terminals, access roads, and parking facilities, while offering continuous service.

Clearing the flight path

One project is an 8,000-foot runway, which should be completed by 2003. The planning department is using ArcView GIS to view and analyze the approach surface (the three-dimensional airspace used by planes as they land).

The planners use the system to find buildings that enter this surface. Some buildings will be removed, some will receive obstruction lights.

In the past, these clearances were calculated using the height of a building's corner closest to the approach surface to determine if it intruded into the flight path and by how much. This approach missed antennas or other building structures that extended higher.

With the GIS, these parts are all accounted for. Using ArcView GIS software's CAD Reader extension, the planners import AutoCAD® files. These files include elevation information about every rooftop structure under the flight path, including heating and cooling devices, parapets, towers, and antennas. Using ArcView 3D Analyst™ and ARC TIN™, the planners can view the approach surfaces to see which buildings are in the flight surface.

Those buildings shown in green will be removed or modified. Those in red will receive an obstruction light.

Clearing the path, part two

With so much construction going on, the same type of analysis has to be done to make sure temporary objects, like cranes, don't intrude into flight surfaces or interfere with the radar beams used to track aircraft.

ArcView 3D Analyst is used to display the three-dimensional flight surfaces and space where the radar beams must pass. Data from construction drawings made with the CAD Reader extension are overlaid on the radar and flight surfaces. Any interferences are shown in green, as indicated at the top of the crane.

The results of this analysis can be viewed in Virtual Reality Modeling Language (VRML), a simulated three-dimensional environment. With a VRML viewer, the analyst can change the viewing perspective by rotating the entire data set to any horizontal and vertical angle. This technology will be especially useful for checking all the airport construction projects that happen simultaneously. Graphics from these analyses are also used by the airport's staff to understand what the airport will look like as new facilities are built. The plans can be rendered for different years and for different scenarios.

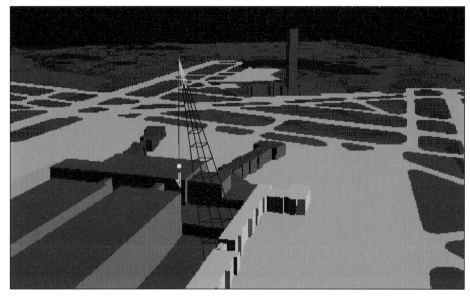

Temporary interferences, such as cranes, can occur during construction on or around airport property.

Good neighbors are quiet neighbors

Construction projects come and go, but GIS is used every day to monitor aircraft noise. Analysts view noise levels at different locations under the flight paths and in nearby areas where people live and work.

About 1,350 planes land or depart daily, generally over densely populated residential areas of Minneapolis.

Residents living here complain about aircraft noise, particularly between 10:30 P.M. and 6 A.M. To please those people—who are after all potential customers—and to meet federal requirements, the airport installs insulation and air conditioners in homes where aircraft noise is loudest.

The GIS helps the analysts identify which homes qualify for this program. With recorded aircraft-noise data, they create DNL (Day Night Level) contours, which describe a blend of scenarios that occur in that airspace. To find the DNL, they use the aircraft decibel level of every plane flying between 10:30 P.M. and 6 A.M. and multiply it by ten—meaning it has ten times the adverse effect of a plane flying in the same place during normal business hours. The result is a set of contours that bulge in certain areas because of night flights.

Noise contours are overlaid in ArcView GIS on parcel data supplied by Hennepin and Dakota counties, where these homes are. The analysts find all of the blocks intersecting these contours and, after summarizing, see that about ten thousand homes will need to be insulated.

Recently, Minnesota's state legislation mandated that the airport expand this program by 2005 to include homes where decibel levels are 60 or higher. The GIS will be used to recalculate the contours.

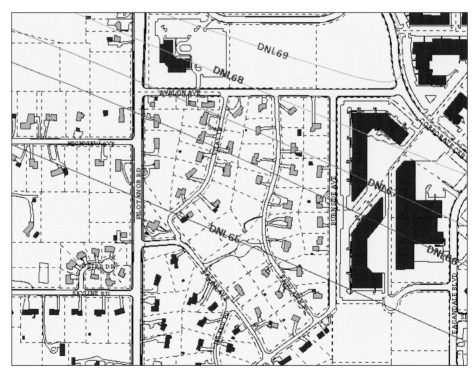

Under new legislation, homes like these, where decibel levels exceed 60, would qualify for MAC's noise-proofing program.

Good neighbors, part two

In addition to insulating homes, airport administrators look for ways to make the noise from departing planes less intrusive in all areas surrounding the airport.

One way has been to direct as many aircraft as possible over the areas southeast of the airport. Zoning in this corridor is mostly commercial and industrial—less sensitive to noise than residential areas.

Last year, they proposed changing the takeoff profile: planes would retract their wing flaps and turn sooner to dampen noise for outlying residential and business areas.

Using ArcView 3D Analyst, they laid the current departure flight track and aircraft noise contours over an orthophoto of land use to see which residences, businesses, and industrial complexes were getting aircraft noise and how loud it was. Next, modeling software was used to calculate the noise levels of the planes if they retracted wing flaps and turned sooner.

This analysis showed that the current takeoff profile affected fewer homes and businesses close to the airport.

Analysts can portray the benefits of two different aircraft approaches, distant and close-in, using the ArcView 3D Analyst extension.

Fifteen thousand complaints

Still, about fifteen thousand complaints are received each year about aircraft noise, so managers must actively investigate them.

Noise data is collected from twenty-four remote monitoring towers and viewed using ArcView Tracking Analyst. The analyst can specify data from a certain time or span of time to see what was happening when the complaint was logged. Perhaps one of the older aircraft was taking off, or a plane was flying too low.

The analyst uses ArcView GIS tools to pan and zoom, or add other data themes to see changes in noise levels. Data from these analyses can determine if noise was unusually high and why, and is used to respond to complaints.

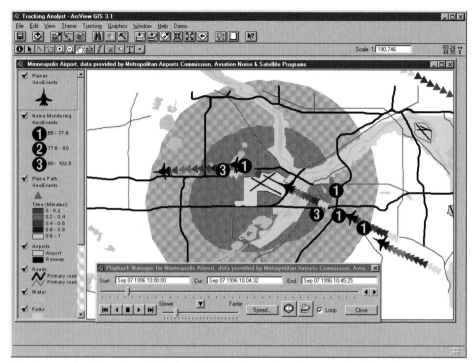

On this map, aircraft are shown in black and noise levels are shown by numerals 1 through 3.

Visit the airport's Web site

As this airport and the cities surrounding it continue to grow, GIS will help keep flight surfaces clear and noise where it's least intrusive.

New maps and data are continually posted to the airport's Web site (www.macavsat.org) and are good examples of how GIS is used for three-dimensional analysis.

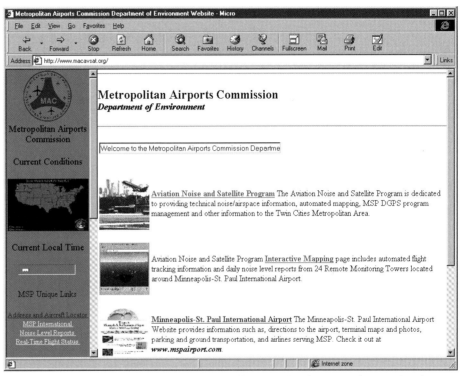

Customers can access the airport's Web site for more information about how GIS is being used in the aviation industry.

Hardware

Sun Ultra™ 1

Sun Ultra 5, 6

SPARCstation™ 20 and 5s

PCs on a LAN

Software

ARC/INFO

Spatial Database Engine™ (SDE™)

ArcView GIS

Oracle®

Data

City of Bloomington

City of Minneapolis

Dakota County

Hennepin County

Metropolitan Council

Metro GIS

Acknowledgments

Thanks to Dan Pfeffer, formerly a GIS specialist in the Aviation Noise Program at the Metropolitan Airports Commission and now the GIS manager at Wenck Associates, an engineering firm in Maple Plain, Minnesota. He can be reached at dpfeffer@wenck.com for more information.

Chapter 8

R i d i n ' t h e r a i l s

For several decades in the nineteenth and twentieth centuries, the railroad was king. It was the fastest, cheapest, most comfortable way to travel or to ship goods. The network symbolically and literally joined by the Golden Spike was perhaps the most ambitious engineering feat of the century, if not the most optimistic. Now frequently bypassed by airplanes and trucks, many railways are rusted, weed-infested tracks leading nowhere.

Many, but by no means all. To compete in today's technological world, some railroads are using GIS to collect and view information about real estate, tracks, locomotives, and railroad cars, making sure everything is profitable and well maintained.

In this chapter, you'll see how Philadelphia-based Consolidated Rail Corporation (Conrail) used GIS to manage its rails and rolling stock, keep the trains running on time, and attract more customers.

From bankruptcy to industry giant

Conrail's origins stretch back to the Granite Railway Company, built in 1826 to carry granite blocks for the Bunker Hill Monument in West Quincy, Massachusetts. Over the following 150 years, scores of northeastern and midwestern railroads were merged into six lines (Central Railroad of New Jersey, Erie Lackawanna, Lehigh & Hudson River, Lehigh Valley, Penn Central, and Reading). By the early 1970s, all had entered bankruptcy, mainly from increasing competition from trucks and from intense federal regulation.

With GIS, Conrail has linked various corporate databases to view information about land, trains, track, cargo, and customers.

In 1976, the federal government created Conrail and upgraded tracks, locomotives, and freight cars. Conrail returned to the private sector in 1987 as a for-profit corporation in what was at the time the largest initial public offering in U.S. history.

By the 1990s, Conrail was an industry giant, serving long-haul and local pickup-and-delivery customers throughout the Northeast and Midwest. Part of its competitive edge came from its use of ARC/INFO to manage spatial information from five divisions. With ArcView GIS, employees and managers throughout the company can access and use the information.

Upgrading tracks, locomotives, and freight cars played a big part in pushing Conrail to the top of the railroad industry.

The sport utility survey cars

Maintenance data about Conrail's locomotives and cars was imported directly into the GIS, but other information, like the position and condition of tracks or lines, had to be collected through a field survey. The engineering department built survey trucks, sport utility vehicles equipped with elevated wheels that allow them to ride down the tracks like a train. The trucks have four computers, a global positioning system (GPS) receiver, a digital camera, a distance counter, and other laser-based surveying equipment.

A two-person crew drives down the rails, collecting position and attribute information for track centerlines, road crossings, turnouts, tunnels, bridges, signals, detectors, lubricators, transponders, and culverts. The raw survey data is processed into ARC/INFO coverages, allowing users to find information about features like road crossings by their location along the line (route measure) as well as their identification number.

Survey trucks ride along the tracks to collect data for the GIS.

Rail wear repair

In the engineering department, which manages things like rails and road-crossing signs, the GIS is used to schedule maintenance and respond to repair requests. As information about rail wear is received, it's entered into the database.

Decisions about which repair jobs to do first are made with tonnage maps, which depict how much weight, or how many cars, travel along the line each day or week. These maps used to be done by hand, using database printouts of train weights (number of cars) and frequencies to calculate tonnage along the lines. The results were color coded and drawn over the rails on a wall map. The wall maps took so long to produce that they were obsolete almost before they were finished.

With the GIS, Conrail's managers click on segments of lines to query the database for their tonnage. This data is displayed on a map. They then overlay locations of reported problems to produce a map showing both repair locations and tonnage. This map is used to decide which repairs to do first.

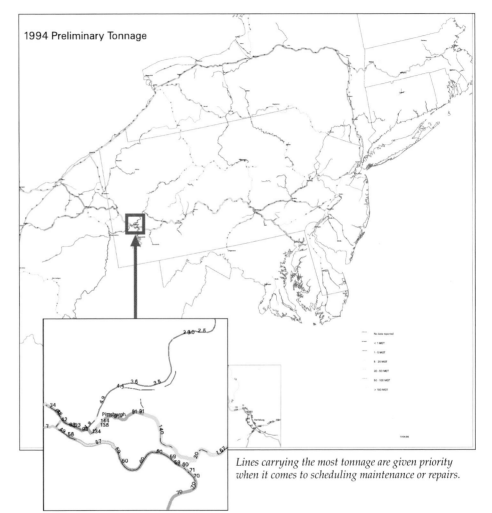

1994 Preliminary Tonnage

Lines carrying the most tonnage are given priority when it comes to scheduling maintenance or repairs.

The slow-order list

When work is being done on the rails, the trains that use those tracks have to slow down, which affects how well the railway performs overall, so another map frequently requested by managers is a slow-order map, which shows where work is being done on the track or where the track is overdue for maintenance.

The vice president of engineering uses slow-order maps in weekly management meetings, so his staff uses ArcView GIS to query the corporate database for Conrail's current slow-order list.

Locations of repair work are geocoded and displayed on the map of the rail lines. The affected track is color coded to show why it's on the list and how long the work will take.

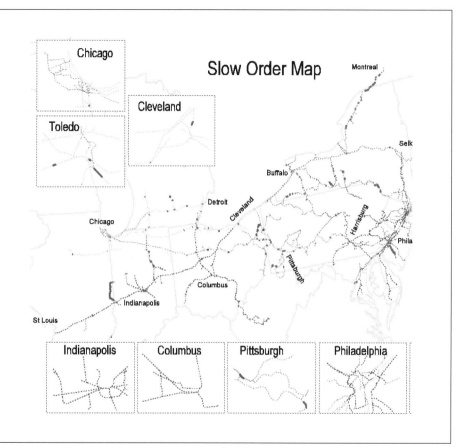

Keeping the trains moving on time is essential to profitability. Slow-order maps help management anticipate delays and determine their duration.

Keep the trains running

Keeping tracks healthy is only part of the picture. Conrail's engineers also use the GIS to help manage the health of the company's twenty-one hundred locomotives—$2 billion worth. Locomotives last an average of seventeen years, with a maximum life expectancy of thirty. The company spends $100 million a year replacing the trains and pushing that average up.

To keep the locomotives in top shape, Conrail's mechanical engineering department designed a system that monitors a locomotive's operating systems (readings from the diesel engine, support systems, and electric systems). An onboard computer collects this information and uploads it by satellite link, along with the locomotive's position, collected by an onboard GPS receiver. The data is sent continuously.

With a GIS, Conrail's maintenance engineers can view the health of locomotives and catch problems like a failing fan early, when they are less costly to repair.

Diagnosis...

In Conrail's headquarters, the data is viewed with ArcView GIS. Positions of the locomotives are shown as green dots if they are operating normally and red if an anomaly is reported by the onboard system, which automatically alerts the Trouble Desk. An operator uses ArcView GIS to see which locomotive is sending the data and where it is as it flashes on the screen.

In a new view the operator has the on-board computer answer diagnostic questions and verify problems. If the engine is running too hot, the data received over the past fifteen minutes, overlaid with information about the track's gradient, might show that the locomotive is pulling uphill. If the engine temperature remained hot where the terrain leveled out, the engine would need to be inspected. The analyst would overlay political boundaries and line ownership to find the nearest place the engine could be checked. With a precise enough diagnosis, the system can also find the closest facility with the necessary parts.

Using ArcView GIS to view data sent by individual locomotives, operators are able to track and monitor each train.

…and cure

ArcView GIS is also used to analyze information received from the onboard systems over time, such as during the past six months or year. In June 1997, for example, when several reports were received from Locomotive 6724 about a digital sensor (used to start the fan that cools the engine), the diagnostic test was inconclusive and no action was taken.

But the problem persisted, so the analyst used ArcView GIS to take another look, viewing the locations of the reports on a map and color coding the icons to represent the time of day and activity associated with each report. In each instance, the locomotive was pulling a heavy load,

sometimes uphill, and was therefore working harder (and hotter). The analyst recommended that Locomotive 6724 be inspected at its next stop. As it turned out, the fuse for a fan controller was blown. Detecting the problem early reduced engine stress and prevented a breakdown.

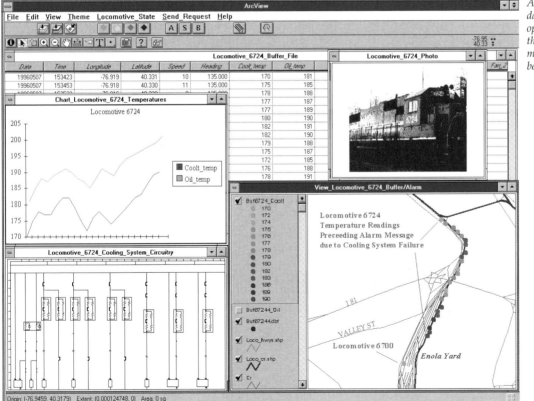

Analyzing various types of data together may give operators the information they need to prevent a minor problem from becoming a disaster.

Train crossing ahead

As a company that crosses paths with the public, literally, Conrail has to care for more than just the well-being of its rails and its trains. That's most obviously true at those places where trains cross roads.

At Conrail, an analyst uses the GIS to query the corporate database for accidents. These are viewed on a map of the lines. Clicking on a crossing's icon calls up its attributes. These show the analyst what signs or lights are there. For many crossings, there are also digital images captured of cars crossing the track after the protective arm has dropped. These have been hotlinked with ArcView GIS to the locations of the crossing so they can be viewed as part of the analysis.

In many cases, adding signs or flashing lights will improve the safety of these intersections; however, it is more difficult to control the daredevils who cross the barriers. But Conrail works with local safety agencies and schools to publicize the dangers of crossing in front of trains.

Rail companies and the federal government use data about where cars are crossing the tracks in front of moving trains to warn drivers of the danger and to decide where to add more warning signs and lights.

Conrail, for all your shipping needs

Beautiful, shiny rails and perfectly running locomotives are worth exactly nothing if no one's using them. So Conrail's marketing staff uses ArcView GIS to search for new customers, businesses that could use the railroad for transporting heavy loads like chemicals or car parts.

Business databases that define key industries by SIC (standard industrial classification) codes are imported into ArcView GIS and plotted on a map. The marketing staff then overlays the rail lines and road network on the map to see which companies are close to the railroad and send them information about Conrail. Should staffers

learn that these companies use a competitor's services, they enter that information into the database. Every few months, they query the database to see which companies use Conrail for shipping and which use competitors. The results are color coded and shown on a map so they can see if Conrail is losing market share or gaining it.

Conrail's marketing staff constantly looks for new customers, querying a database to find out which local companies are using competitors.

GIS standards for the entire industry

In 1999, two other rail companies, CSX and Norfolk Southern, will divide Conrail between them. They will continue some of the current GIS development by combining these efforts with their own projects. Conrail will continue operating freight services within New Jersey, Philadelphia, and Detroit, and will use GIS to manage the lines and locomotives it owns. The company will also continue its work with the Association of American Railroads and other agencies to develop GIS standards for the railroad industry.

Though the future of its GIS program is uncertain, Conrail has pioneered many applications unique at this time in its industry.

Hardware

UNIX® servers and workstations

PCs

Software

ARC/INFO

ArcView GIS

Spatial Database Engine (SDE)

Data

Conrail proprietary data

GDT Dynamap/2000®

Bureau of Transportation statistics

U.S. Bureau of the Census data

Other data specific to internal analysis projects

Acknowledgments

Thanks to the following individuals at Conrail: Todd Crane, former manager of GIS development; Stephen Sullivan, director of corporate planning; and Robert Libkind, director of media relations.

CONRAIL

Chapter 9

Trains on track

While more and more people are taking trains to work, the convenience of driving one's own car is still so great as to override even the pain of negotiating traffic jams and the guilt of polluting the air. To reduce gridlock and air pollution, and make enough money to stay in business, commuter rail companies have to offer consistently fast and reliable service.

In this chapter, you'll see how the Tri-County Commuter Rail Authority (Tri-Rail), a commuter train service in South Florida, keeps its trains running on time.

Wooing commuters

Tri-Rail in South Florida offers twenty-eight trips a day between West Palm Beach and Miami Airport. In recent years, the number of passengers has dropped, even though the number of people in the area has increased. People complained that the trains weren't consistently on time.

In 1996, Tri-Rail asked GeoFocus, a GIS developer in Gainesville, Florida, to demonstrate a GIS-based train-tracking system to show where the trains were and how long before they'd arrive at the next station.

In 1997, GeoFocus delivered TrainTrac, a GIS built with MapObjects software. The system runs on a server at the train operations center in Hialeah, Florida, and links with Tri-Rail's customer service center in Hialeah.

Each train broadcasts its position to the operations center so it can be tracked and passengers kept informed of arrival times.

Open lines of communication

Computers on each train have built-in global positioning system (GPS) receivers and 900-MHz wireless modems that report the train's identification number, latitude and longitude, and speed to the operations center.

This data is displayed on a map that shows where trains are and how their performance compares to published schedules.

Through the onboard computer, the operations center lets the train crews know about speed restrictions, track blockages, construction, and emergencies. Information about train delays and arrival times is updated on the message boards at the station platforms.

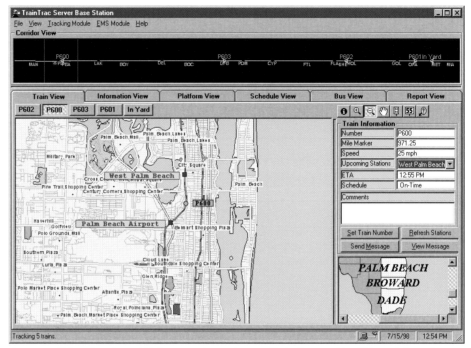

Operators click on the tabs to shift from one view to the next. Each view provides different information about each train.

P604 is on time for Golden Glades

The same data is used by the operators in the customer service center who answer telephone inquiries about train arrivals, departures, and connections to Tri-Rail buses. The idea was to eliminate as much paper as possible from their desks and broaden the type of information they could relay to callers.

A call comes in to the customer service center about Train P604. An operator uses the Train View tab in TrainTrac to see where it is and tell the caller when it's estimated to arrive.

P604 has left the Hollywood Station. The view shows the train's position and speed, and its estimated time of arrival (ETA) for the next station, Golden Glades. The train's color, in this case, green, indicates it's on time. A train five minutes behind will be yellow, and ten minutes behind or more, red.

The operator can use Train View's pull-down menus to provide ETAs for other stations or can select a different train number to see its location, speed, and ETAs.

By selecting P604, the operator sees its location along the line (in the red circle) and below in more detail.

Doing the commute

A caller wants to use the Mangonia Park station to travel south to Deerfield Beach on weekday mornings. With TrainTrac's Schedule View tab, the operator can give departure times from the station. Selecting a particular station as a destination, like Boca Raton or Hollywood, gives return times. Many callers ask how much the trip will cost, so the tab shows the fare for the selections entered.

Because some passengers are connecting with Tri-Rail's shuttle buses, the operator can use the Bus View tab to view shuttle bus schedules, trip fares, and other information, such as route stop addresses and directions to bus stops.

TrainTrac Server Base Station

File View Tracking Module EMS Module Help

Corridor View

Schedule View — Weekday South

Station	P601	P603	P605	P607	P609	P611	P613	P615	P617	P619	P621	P623	P625	P627
Mangonia Park	4:20	5:18	-----	6:29	7:49	9:12	10:17	11:28	1:55	3:09	4:39	5:32	7:00	7:57
West Palm Beach	4:27	5:25	6:01	6:36	7:56	9:19	10:24	11:35	2:02	3:16	4:46	5:39	7:07	8:04
Palm Beach Airport	4:31	5:29	6:04	6:40	8:00	9:23	10:28	11:39	2:06	3:20	4:50	5:43	7:11	8:08
Lake Worth	4:38	5:36	6:11	6:47	8:11	9:36	10:35	11:46	2:13	3:27	4:57	5:50	7:21	8:15
Boynton Beach	4:44	5:42	6:16	6:53	8:17	9:42	10:41	11:52	2:19	3:33	5:02	5:56	7:26	8:21
Delray Beach	4:53	5:52	6:24	7:03	8:26	9:51	10:51	12:01	2:29	3:42	5:10	6:06	7:35	8:30
Boca Raton	4:59	5:58	6:29	7:09	8:32	9:57	10:57	12:07	2:35	3:48	5:15	6:12	7:41	8:36
Deerfield Beach	5:06	6:05	6:36	7:16	8:39	10:04	11:04	12:14	2:42	3:55	5:22	6:19	7:48	8:43
Pompano Beach	5:11	6:10	6:41	7:21	8:44	10:09	11:09	12:19	2:47	4:00	5:27	6:24	7:53	8:48
Cypress Creek	5:19	6:19	6:50	7:30	8:52	10:17	11:17	12:28	2:55	4:08	5:35	6:32	8:01	8:56
Fort Lauderdale	5:29	6:30	7:00	7:40	9:02	10:27	11:27	12:38	3:05	4:18	5:45	6:42	8:11	9:06
Fort Lauderdale Airport	5:36	6:37	7:07	7:47	9:09	10:34	11:34	12:45	3:12	4:25	5:52	6:49	8:18	9:13
Sheridan Street	5:39	6:41	7:11	7:50	9:12	10:37	11:37	12:49	3:15	4:28	5:55	6:52	8:21	9:16
Hollywood	5:43	6:45	7:14	7:54	9:16	10:41	11:41	12:53	3:19	4:32	5:59	6:56	8:25	9:20
Golden Glades	5:53	6:55	7:24	8:03	9:25	10:50	11:50	1:02	3:28	4:41	6:08	7:05	8:35	9:30
Opa-Locka	5:58	7:00	7:29	8:08	9:30	10:55	11:55	1:07	3:33	4:46	6:13	7:10	8:40	9:35
Metrorail Transfer	6:06	7:08	7:42	8:16	9:38	11:03	12:03	1:15	3:41	4:55	6:22	7:18	8:48	9:43
Hialeah Market	6:11	7:13	-----	8:21	9:43	11:08	12:08	1:20	3:46	5:00	6:27	7:23	8:53	9:48
Miami Airport	6:20	7:22	-----	8:30	9:52	11:17	12:17	1:29	3:55	5:09	6:36	7:32	9:02	9:57

Ticket Type [Round Trip]   Travel Time [44 min.]   Total Fare [$6.75]

Tracking 4 trains.   8/17/98   8:43 AM

The Schedule View allows the operator to quickly refer to train schedules and provide information on trip fares.

Train status

As the information comes in from the trains, their location and status display on a map. When trains are running late, their status is sent to their next stations.

These messages are displayed at the stations and broadcast through a public-address system in both English and Spanish.

Under the Platform View tab, the operator sees which messages are being displayed and broadcast and can change a message by choosing another one or by typing one in when something out of the ordinary happens, like a blocked track or an accident.

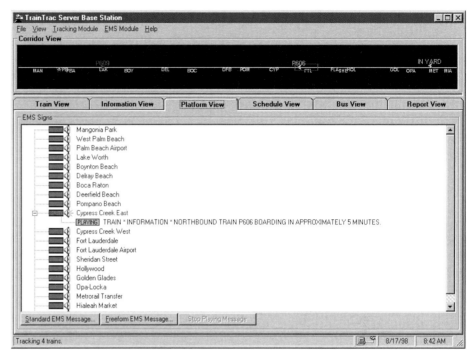

By selecting Cypress Creek East, the operator sees the message being broadcast at that station.

Performance reviews

Tracking-system operators use the Information View tab to keep track of the trains' performance compared to the schedule.

Performance information, summarized under the Report View tab, shows which trains are consistently on time and which aren't. This summary of train arrivals and departures helps operations managers find out if schedules should be adjusted to help the trains stay on time.

Recently, the GIS has been used to make information about train schedules, ETAs, and shuttle bus connections available to the public. Using a touch-tone phone, customers choose from menus to find where a specific train is or to listen to the schedule of ETAs for a station.

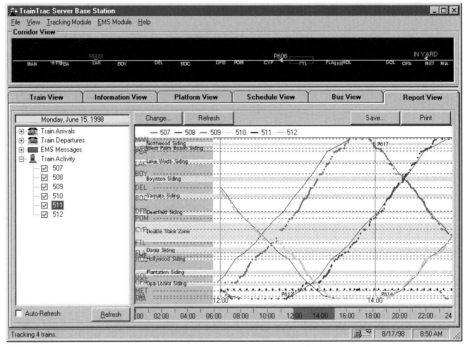

This time plot is generated in the Report View to show train positions in relation to time over a specified period, in this case two hours.

Automated customer paging

In the future, Tri-Rail plans to use MapObjects Internet Map Server technology to provide information about train locations on the Internet so passengers can determine when the train is ten or fifteen minutes from a station.

Tri-Rail hopes that by giving their current passengers reliable information about when the trains will arrive, the word will spread, and more business travelers and tourists will want to use Tri-Rail's trains and shuttle buses.

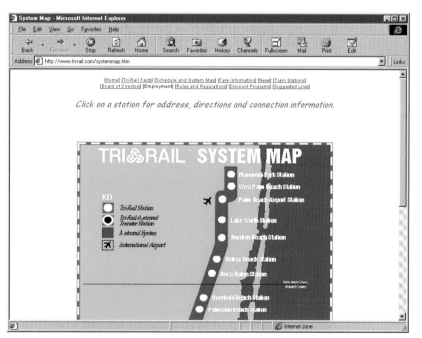

With passengers able to find train schedules, bus schedules, and more on the Internet, Tri-Rail hopes more people will opt to ride its trains.

Hardware

IBM-compatible computers using
Windows 95, Windows 98®, and
Windows NT operating systems

Software

MapObjects

MapObjects LT

Microsoft Visual Basic® version 5.0

Data

Real-time positional data is gathered from
GPS receivers, 900-MHz wireless, data
modems, station electronic message
controller units, and local area network
interface.

Acknowledgments

Thanks to Les Nehiley, project manager,
signal and communications, Tri-County
Commuter Rail Authority, and to Dwain
Jenkins, mobile computing business unit
manager, GeoFocus, Inc.

Chapter 10

Come wind, come snow

It is an idyllic picture. So calm and peaceful and romantic that it has appeared on countless magazine covers and greeting cards—snow. Snow covering lakes and fields, snow covering hedges and fences. Unfortunately, it also covers roads and bridges where people want to drive. Along with ice, snow makes these surfaces dangerous and sometimes impassable.

It is a heroic picture. It doesn't make it onto greeting cards or magazine covers, but there it is. Every winter, men and women in parkas and scarves with their mighty snowplows, out in the cold and the wind to keep the roads clear for all of us sitting cozily by the fire, sipping hot tea and planning holiday outings.

In this chapter, you'll seen how Virginia's Department of Transportation uses GIS technology and global positioning system (GPS) receivers to keep its snowplows running, its drivers safe, and the roads clear.

14,000 miles to plow...

Fairfax County, Virginia, doesn't get much snow by the standards of Michigan or Minnesota, but what it gets can freeze traffic in and out of the nation's capital for days and cost millions to remove.

Virginia's Department of Transportation is responsible for plowing the roads leading in and out of Washington, D.C. Counting each lane separately (and they do), that comes to some 14,000 miles to plow. In 1996, after spending $44 million to clear the roads, the department decided it was time to save some money.

With GPS-equipped snowplows, the operations center is able to send immediate help when there's an emergency.

...and eighty snowplows to plow them

They started by improving communications. In 1997, they installed an Automatic Vehicle Location (AVL) unit in eighty snowplows. Each unit, which looks like an overgrown pager, plugs into the plow's cigarette lighter. Each unit has a GPS receiver, a two-way messaging system, a wireless modem, a four-button keypad, and an interface to the snowplow's sensors. Every thirty seconds, it sends the snowplow's latitude and longitude to the district center in Merrifield, along with the status of the sensor, so dispatchers and supervisors can monitor them as they work.

Using data entered by each driver, operators at the district center can see where the trucks are and what they're doing.

Truck tracker

Each truck's position is viewed and ana-
lyzed using MapObjects. The map of Fairfax County shows primary roads as thick
lines, secondary roads as thin lines, and
snowplows as circled dots. Above each
truck is a box displaying its ID, how much
salt or sand it has spread, the rate of
spread (in pounds per mile), and the temperature of both road and air.

As the trucks drive through the streets, a
trace appears behind each, color coded to
indicate whether its plow or spreader is
being used and if the engine is running.

If a truck makes a wrong turn or isn't
spreading salt when it should, the system
alerts the operator and centers that truck
on the display.

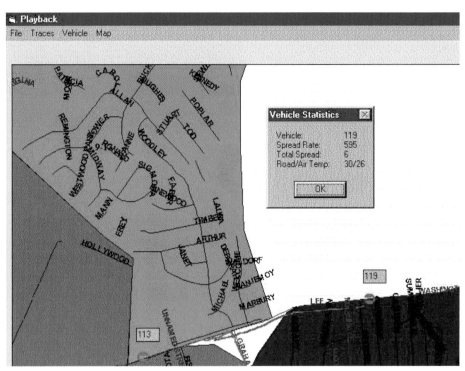

Users set the elapsed time (in minutes), width, and color for the trace from pull-down menus.

Salt spreader

A truck has stopped spreading salt too early along its route. The operator clicks on its icon and then on the Send Message button and selects "Start spreading" from the on-screen choices. The operator could also type a message like "Proceed to Route 21 and begin spreading at 500 pounds/lane mile."

If the truck driver has received and understood the message, the next sensor update will show the truck's dot as green.

If there was no response or the in-cab emergency button was pressed, the GIS would show the operator the three closest trucks with lines drawn from each to show its distance from the truck in trouble.

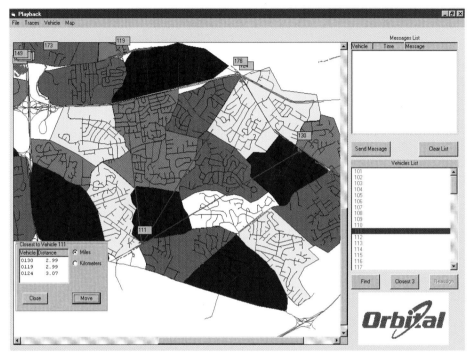

The system shows operators the truck in trouble and the three closest vehicles to that location so they can send help and reassign the route.

Plow and plow again

The GIS keeps track of more than snow-plows. It keeps track of the roads as well. Each road along the regular routes has to be plowed or salted at regular intervals, sometimes as often as every hour. The frequency a road should be cleared is attached to it in the attribute table.

The GIS automatically tracks these elapsed times as the trucks clear the roads. The track changes color as it ages. The road shown here in green will age to red over the next two hours, at which time it will have to be replowed or resalted. If the snowplow on this route is running behind or becomes disabled, the dispatcher will be able to send another truck to clear this road.

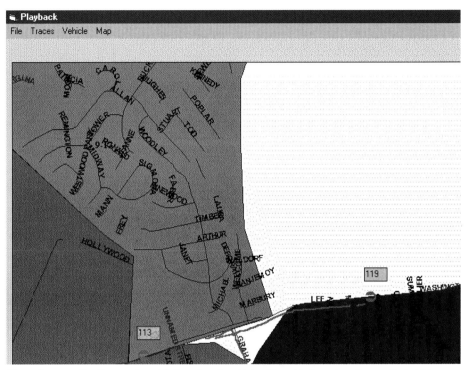

Dispatchers monitor the map to watch for red roads, which will need to be replowed or resalted right away.

Full disclosure

All of this information is available to the public. If someone calls to ask how soon a road will be cleared, the dispatcher can enter the street name or an address to zoom to the zone that it's in, in this case zone 2-04. The display shows which streets have been cleared or soon will be.

To confirm that the snowplow scheduled to plow a street is indeed on its way, the dispatcher can double-click on the truck's symbol on the GIS map to see its statistics box. The map centers on that snowplow and zooms to it.

Between the message list and the map, the dispatcher gets a pretty complete picture of what's happening. In this case, the snowplow has returned to base to replenish its salt and will have that road cleared within two hours.

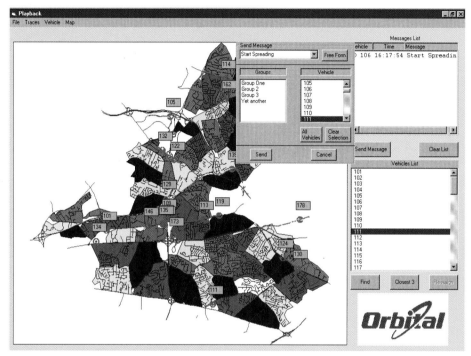

Eventually, the snow center in Fairfax will use the GIS data to make maps for the media to be posted to the Internet or broadcast on the county's cable channel.

Efficiency experts

The data, which is maintained in Microsoft Access, is studied to see how to make the department more efficient.

The supervisor can look at individual trucks or all of the trucks working in a zone to see which ones complete their routes on time, and can use this information to adjust the routes, adding more streets to some and less to others, to look for a balance that would help drivers get the routes done faster.

Another query might be to look at how much salt each vehicle spreads per mile and compare the spread statistics to see if some drivers are not spreading enough or are spreading too much.

The supervisor can also use the data to see how much material is being used by all trucks and estimate how much is being spent to clear the streets per hour, per day, or per storm, and can then use this information to justify budget figures.

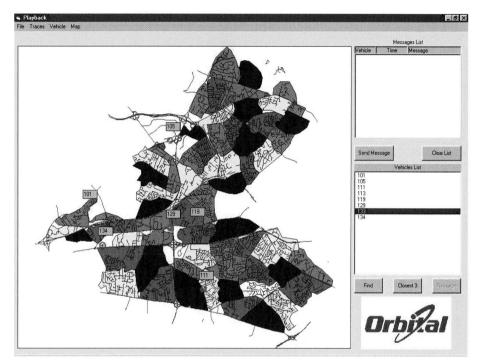

The system's Playback feature allows the department to view where the trucks are at any given time.

Knocking mailboxes over

Even the most efficient operations aren't perfect. Headquarters has just received a call complaining that a snowplow knocked a mailbox over, either yesterday or the day before. The supervisor clicks on the Playback button and enters the address, date, and start and stop times. The system zooms to the location and plays back the sequence of the trucks in that area at that time. The statistics box shows that truck 119 was on the road, yesterday and the day before. That doesn't mean that truck 119 knocked the box down, but at least the supervisor can ask the right driver for more information. This helps with both liability management and driver accountability.

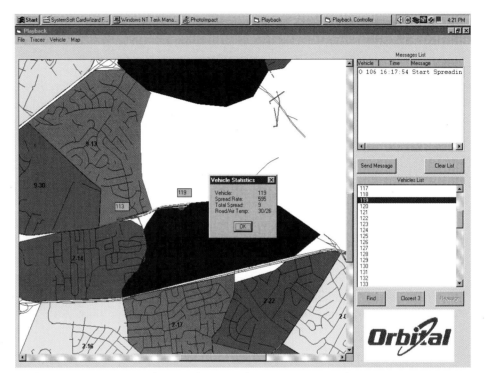

Headquarters can monitor records to see where snowplows were on a certain day.

MapObjects and GPS for the whole fleet

After the wind has died down and the snow has melted away, there's still work to do. The department is looking to expand the use of MapObjects and GPS to other counties and equip its line-painting trucks and other vehicles to increase their efficiency as well.

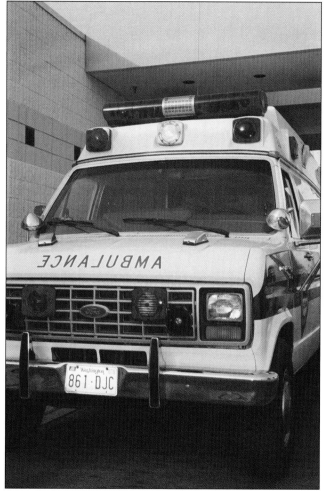

The system could be adapted for the needs of tracking other types of vehicles, including street sweepers, paint trucks, ambulances, and fire trucks.

Hardware

ORBTRAC-100, from Orbital Sciences Corporation, in vehicles

Pentium® PCs at the operations center

Software

MapObjects

Microsoft Access

Data

MAPTEK street data

Real-time GPS positions

Sensor data from snowplows

Acknowledgments

Thanks to Chris Body and John Leatherman of Orbital Sciences Corporation, Germantown, Maryland.

• • • • • •
Keep it moving

When you're stuck at a city stoplight with no turn lane, waiting to make a left onto a main street, cars spaced just far enough apart to be really annoying, traffic can seem pretty constant. It's not. That steady flow that has you fuming at 4:30 in the afternoon was a mere trickle at 2:55 in the morning. Out in the suburbs, traffic might be light all day except for mornings and evenings.

Uneven traffic is not something traffic signals of the past were designed to handle. In fact, heavy traffic could be made much worse by signals that plod from green to yellow to red at the same evenly spaced intervals.

In this chapter, you'll see how Oakland County in Michigan uses GIS and a video traffic management system to set traffic lights to change according to traffic flow, making traffic smoother and safer, and drivers calmer and more serene.

The search for alternatives

Oakland County, Michigan, is one of the fastest growing counties in the nation. Its road commission maintains 2,600 miles of county roads, over 310 miles of state highways, and more than 1,200 traffic signals.

In the mid-1980s, officials realized they wouldn't have enough money to build new roads or widen existing ones fast enough to keep pace with the county's increasing traffic.

The traffic signals of today adjust to traffic flow, allowing for safer streets and calmer drivers.

From buried sensors to sensors on sticks

Their search for alternatives to traditional road construction led them to Sydney, Australia. In the 1970s, Sydney was faced with a similar situation—too much traffic and not enough roads. The Road and Traffic Authority of New South Wales developed a system of sensors buried in the pavement at intersections to collect information about traffic flow and control traffic signals. These sensors also serve as triggers for red-light cameras.

Road Commission for Oakland County (RCOC) officials were so impressed with Sydney's system that, in 1991, they installed one of their own based on it. Called FAST-TRAC, Oakland County's system was the first of its kind in America and is still the largest.

Because sensors in the pavement like those used in Sydney would require more maintenance, RCOC decided to use camera-like devices attached to poles to collect data about traffic volume.

Intersections like this one needed traffic flow management beyond just a time-regulated traffic signal.

Autoscope cameras

These digital imaging systems, called Autoscope™ cameras, detect approaching vehicles and transmit the information about traffic flow to a computer in a control box at the intersection. These computers send the information to one of five regional computers, which automatically adjust the traffic signals, lengthening or shortening the time red or green stays on in any direction.

The regional computers also keep traffic flowing along major corridors. As traffic increases, these computers adjust traffic lights to keep cars moving. These computers are connected to a central management computer at a Traffic Operations Center, which also receives data from regional bus systems, local police departments, and the Michigan Department of Transportation.

Instead of in-pavement sensors, FAST-TRAC uses digital imaging cameras to capture data for calculating the volume of approaching vehicles.

The video wall

All the traffic data is stored in an Informix® database and is used by RCOC's other traffic management systems, including an ArcView GIS extension built by Odetics ITS (Anaheim, California) and subcontractor Ground Control (Fayetteville, North Carolina) to view the data and query it.

This extension, called TIMS (for Transportation Information Management System), reads the Informix database every five minutes (or more, at the operator's discretion) and displays the results in ArcView GIS on an operator workstation. The extension allows operators to input data like the location of an incident or traffic event. The operator can then populate data elements, such as the number of lanes affected or a location description. All of the data is maintained through the TIMS programs and displayed in the ArcView GIS map display.

The screens can show the whole area or different parts of it. They show the roads, the locations of the sensors (shown as traffic lights), and the locations of the closed-circuit TV (CCTV) cameras operated by RCOC and the Michigan Department of Transportation. Their video feeds are shared by all the agencies.

GIS data can be displayed on the terminals or on the video wall, depending on who needs to view the action.

Monitoring congestion

At the center's four workstations, operators view the real-time data for the FAST-TRAC system.

Congestion is shown as differently colored arrows (from green for not congested, through yellow and orange, to red for very congested). The map displayed is updated automatically.

Operators have access to the camera control, which allows them to display the live video on a PC, the video wall, or any of the twelve monitors around the wall. Users can access this camera control by clicking on the camera they want to see.

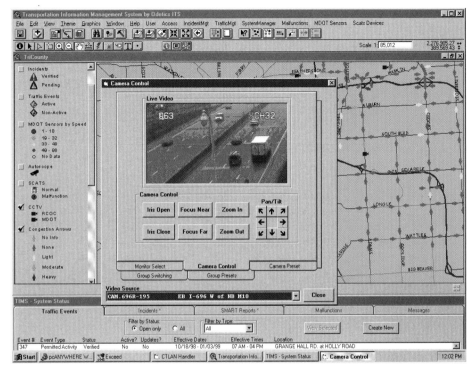

Zooming in on the action via CCTV helps operators understand why traffic has stopped and send help if it's needed.

Finding the antidote

The image doesn't show any obvious reason for traffic slowing down, so the operator looks at the Traffic Events layer, which includes information about road construction, concerts, ball games, parades—anything that they would know about ahead of time that could affect traffic.

The application displays active and inactive events. For example, a construction project may only be worked on between 9 A.M. and 4 P.M. to avoid rush hours. When the time of day is within that time window, the event will display as active; otherwise, it displays as inactive.

Because nothing's happening along this corridor, and nothing's planned, the operator goes to Freeway Speeds to see what's happening there.

A nearby freeway is congested from an accident. Apparently, surface streets are becoming congested as people exit the freeway to avoid it. In the TIMS application, the operator updates the Informix database with the reason the surface street is congested and how long that situation is likely to last.

Events like road construction, ball games, and concerts are programmed into the system so the operator can see where they are and how long they will last. Incidents like accidents and other traffic problems are entered using the dialog screen.

Live weather, and more

The agency plans to integrate a live weather feed into FAST-TRAC, reporting temperature, precipitation, and other weather information. This data will be collected at the Traffic Center and viewed on the traffic maps. It could be used to plan snowplow routes and announce road conditions.

FAST-TRAC will also integrate TIMS with the freeway management system being used by the Michigan Department of Transportation (MDOT). MapObjects was used to build this system. When MDOT's video cameras identify a change in traffic conditions, both agencies (RCOC and MDOT) could advise motorists about what to do, MDOT with message signs and RCOC on its Web site where the agency is using ArcView Internet Map Server (IMS) to make real-time traffic data available. ArcView Network Analyst, another ArcView GIS extension, will be used by RCOC in the future to provide an Internet route-planning system.

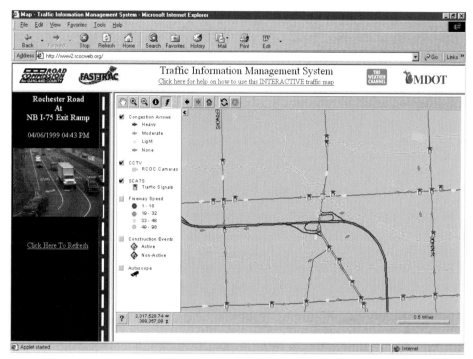

In the very near future, drivers will check traffic conditions over the Internet, planning routes around areas where there are accidents or events causing congestion.

Hardware

Windows NT workstations

Windows NT server-based Web server

Sun Ultra database server

Software

ArcView GIS

ArcView IMS

Informix

TIMS extension for ArcView GIS

ARC/INFO

Data

SCATS sensor data

CCTV

Bus data

Traffic accident data

Highway data

Acknowledgments

Thanks to Gary Piotrowicz of the Road Commission for Oakland County; Doug Ruppel of Ground Control; and Jeff Manring of Odetics ITS in Madison Heights, Michigan.

Ground Control

www.grndctrl.com

Chapter 12

In good repair

The roads we drive, the bridges we cross, the signs and signals that guide us—they all deteriorate over time. So they all need to be kept in constant repair. New roads and new bridges need to be built. New signals need to be put up to cut down on accidents. In a state like Missouri, with thousands of bridges and tens of thousands of roads, and several divisions within the transportation department, building and repair schedules need to be carefully coordinated to make sure that the right things get done at the right time.

In this chapter, you'll see how engineers in Missouri's Department of Transportation use GIS to find and analyze data to keep roads, bridges, and signs in good repair.

Sixth largest in the United States

The Missouri Department of Transportation (MoDOT), headquartered in Jefferson City, maintains 8,000 bridges and 32,000 miles of highway. That's the sixth largest highway system in the United States, and it's spread over 70,000 square miles. Ten MoDOT district offices design and build bridges and highways, widen roads, and maintain traffic signs and lights. Because all projects are approved by Jefferson City, it's important for headquarters staff to understand local traffic issues and work closely with the districts in planning changes.

Using their GIS, Missouri DOT's engineers can find information about any intersection or stretch of highway in the state.

Coordinated data

During the 1980s, information on the highways and bridges was automated with various computer-aided design (CAD) systems. In 1995, the department formed the Transportation Management System Division to coordinate the spatial information from the Bridge, Safety, Traffic, and Congestion divisions. This data was distributed, along with several ArcView GIS applications, to about five hundred employees.

Engineers in the DOT's divisions use the GIS to find and analyze information, and submit changes to Jefferson City where the data is maintained in an Oracle database.

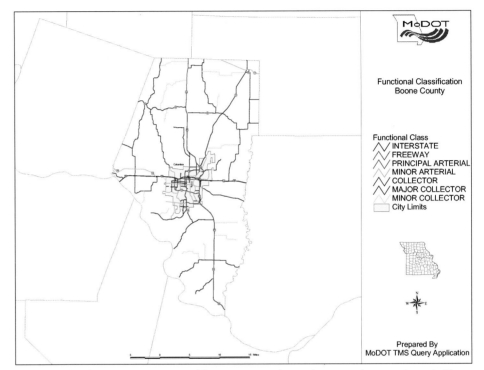

The system has about sixty preprogrammed buttons to create frequently requested maps and reports like functional class maps of Missouri's roads and highways.

Smoothing out the roads

In District 6, motorists have been complaining about rough pavement on the interstate. A highway engineer goes to the District 6 basemap in the GIS to see where the roughness has been reported. Surface roughness and cracks are duly noted, along with the date of the last inspection.

Querying the system for a digital image of the spot shows faint lines where traffic has been diverted recently, probably when the bridge on the other side of the highway was improved.

Checking the schedule for other improvements in the county shows that the lanes in question are set to be resurfaced and painted the following week. The people can be informed that their road will soon be smooth again.

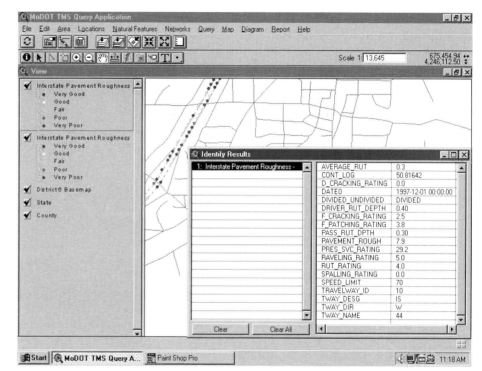

Using ArcView GIS software's Identify command, the engineer selects a road segment to view detailed information about its pavement.

Keeping bridges safe

Bridges in the state are inspected yearly and rated as excellent, good, fair, poor, or defective. A bridge engineer uses this data to schedule improvements for the coming year. The engineer starts by creating a map of the defective bridges in each county and then uses ArcView GIS software's Identify command to view information about each bridge, when it was built, when it was last inspected, traffic volume (current and forecast), how long it is, and how many lanes it has. Bridges with more traffic will be recommended first for repair.

The bridge data is also used to prepare the National Bridge Inventory, an annual report that provides inspection information to the United States Department of Transportation about all key bridges in each state.

Using the system's query menus, engineers create summary reports and maps of the state's bridges by county, condition, or type. On the map, the red segment is of concern so the engineer uses the GIS to view a digital image of the bridge and highway lanes.

It's a good sign

In addition to tracking information about Missouri's highways and bridges, MoDOT tracks data about signs and signals. An engineer uses the GIS to find information about parts of a traffic signal that need to be replaced. Clicking on the signal or entering its ID number shows its date of installation, type of standard, type of

controller (such as a timed controller), manufacturer, and when it was last inspected. The engineer can view digital photos of the signals to see how the lights are mounted and query the system to find out how many signals from the same manufacturer are in a county or in the state and where they are located.

The inventory in the GIS shows whether the district office has these parts. If not, the engineer can order them from the manufacturer. When the new parts are delivered, an electronic work order is sent to the district so the old parts can be replaced.

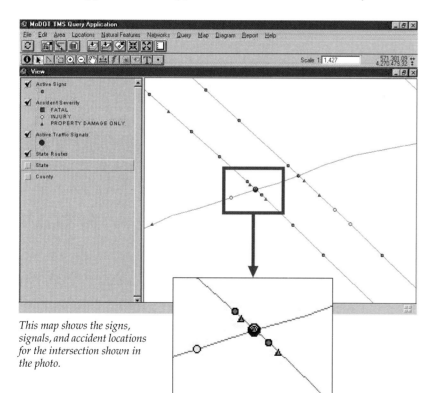

This map shows the signs, signals, and accident locations for the intersection shown in the photo.

Accident prevention

The department monitors accident data closely to make sure all the signs and signals are doing their job of keeping drivers out of each other's way.

One engineer uses the system to query for the location of fatal accidents during the past year. Areas with higher fatality rates are made a priority for further inspection and, if necessary, repair or redesign.

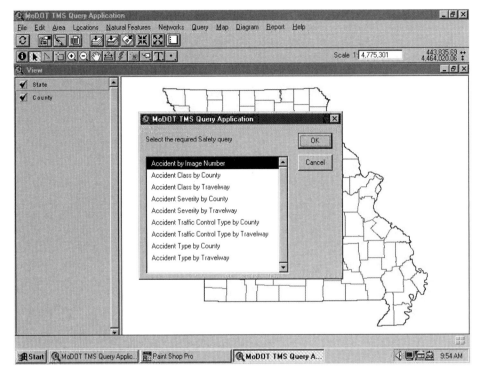

The Safety Query menu is used to quickly find and map accident data by county, severity, or type.

Deer crossing

Another engineer queries the system for traffic accidents involving deer. Many occur near a cornfield where deer graze. The engineer recommends placing a reflective sign here.

Overlaying deer accident data from 1994 (when the speed limit was 55 miles per hour) and 1997 (when it was 70) shows more accidents in 1997, so the engineer recommends lowering the speed limit along these segments in addition to the new sign.

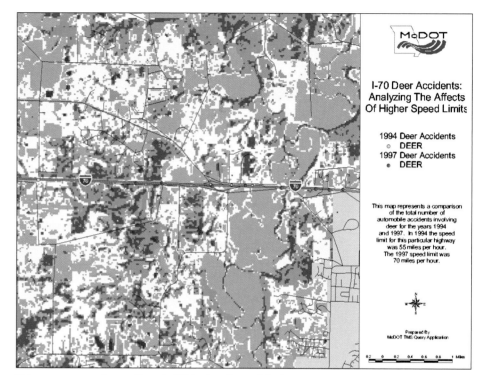

This map compares deer accidents in 1994, when the speed limit was 55 MPH, and in 1997, when the limit was raised to 70.

Accurate inventories

Each year, managers use the system to check the accuracy of the roadway inventories submitted by Missouri's 115 counties for federal funding. With the GIS, they look at each county's roads by type (state highway, arterial, subarterial) and summarize their mileage. The results are compared to the records provided by the counties. If there are discrepancies, they overlay the county's road and highway themes with their own to identify roads that may have been overlooked. Once the county records are verified, they are sent on.

The system also lets managers tally roads by political boundaries, so they can make a map of improvement projects in congressional districts or by city boundaries. These maps and data are frequently requested by local politicians, lobbyists, and the media.

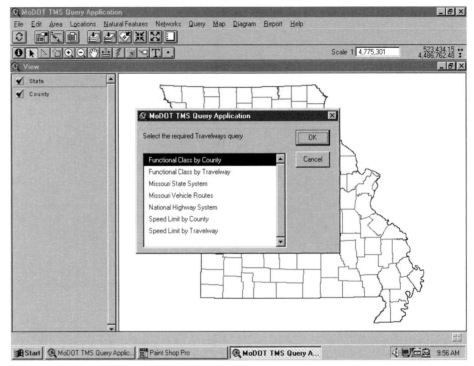

Managers used the system to verify data sent by counties and create maps of highways by their functional class, state or federal designation, or speed limit.

Publishing on the Internet

The department hopes to make driving in Missouri even more safe and pleasant by using Internet Map Server software from ESRI to publish GIS data about road conditions and repair schedules.

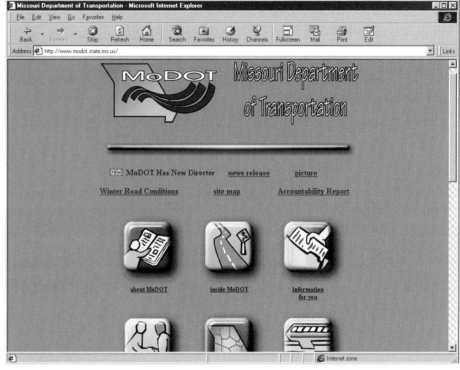

The Missouri DOT plans to publish highway data on its Internet Web site so tourists, commuters, and business travelers can plan driving trips and print their own maps and reports.

Hardware

Windows NT workstations (ArcView GIS)

IBM UNIX server (ARC/INFO)

Software

ArcView GIS

Oracle

ARC/INFO

Data

Roadway maintenance, signs, lighting, bridges, pavement, congestion management, safety management, and intermodal facilities (aviation, waterways, transit, and rail) data

Supplemental coverages of hydrology, geology, demographic, business, and political data

Acknowledgments

Thanks to Tony Perkins and Darren Williams of Missouri DOT's Transportation Management Systems Division, and to Kevin Howard of GIS/Trans, Ltd.

Chapter 13

Over the river and through the town

In large cities, the streets or highways you choose can make all the difference between getting to your destinations on time, and in a good mood, and being late to everything and having a migraine to boot. It's no help to know that while traffic could be blocked for hours along the route you choose, it could be moving pretty freely on others. Traffic reports on radio or television are good only for when they're broadcast, and only for selected streets.

In this chapter, you'll see how the Korea Road Traffic Information Centre in Seoul, South Korea, uses GIS to provide drivers with news about traffic conditions, the weather, and route planning—always current, for all streets, all over the Internet.

Putting drivers on the map

About twenty-seven million people live in the South Korean capital of Seoul and the cities around it. Most business and commercial centers are located in the downtown area to the north of the Han river, while many workers live south of it. Their daily commute to work averages one and a half hours, complicated by having to cross the Han. While seventeen bridges span the Han, choosing the wrong one on the wrong day, if there's road work or an accident, can add hours to the drive.

In Seoul, high-volume traffic is complicated by limited access to the city from residential areas via seventeen bridges crossing the Han river.

www.kortic.or.kr

Three years ago, Korea's Road Traffic Safety Authority and National Police Agency formed the Korea Road Traffic Information Centre. The Centre has developed a system that provides traffic information to commuters, tourists, and businesses in the Seoul area. Its Web site provides information on traffic jams, crashes, delays, road work, and weather. Hundreds of people log on to this site daily to check current traffic conditions and plan their driving route.

The Web site is in Korean, but there is an English translation for information on road sections, bridges, tunnels, and intersections.

Putting drivers on the map

Using the Web site

A commuter living southeast of Seoul uses the Centre's Web site to decide which bridge to use to cross the Han River that day. Selecting Local Traffic Information for Seoul from the opening screen displays the city's roads in green, yellow, and red.

Seeing that traffic is moving fast at the Seoul tunnel or Anjuro bridge, the commuter asks for other traffic information. Clicking on PathSearch gives a choice between Shortest Path or Optimal Search to have the system plan a driving route. Shortest Path calculates the route by distance alone. Optimal Search figures in current traffic speeds, road work, and accidents.

All our hypothetical commuter has to do now is enter the locations where the trip will start and finish, or select them on the map. The system performs the calculations and provides a route map and driving directions. Before printing this map, other data like parking lots, gas stations, and auto repair shops can be added. The site also provides links to airlines, public transit, and other intelligent transportation system (ITS) systems.

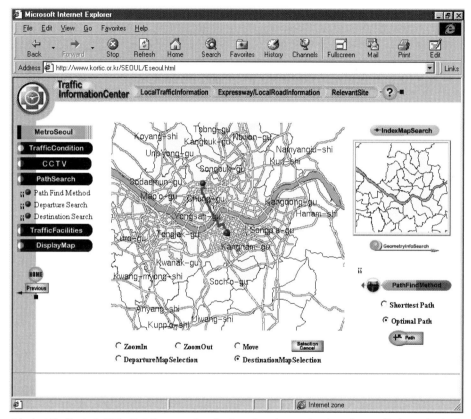

A look at the Centre's Web site tells commuters, business travelers, or tourists where traffic is moving and where it's stalled.

Chapter 13   Over the river and through the town

113

Commercial applications

The online maps and traffic data benefit all drivers in Seoul, not just commuters. Companies with fleets of vehicles, for instance, use the system to route their trucks, ambulances, or delivery vans.

An ambulance service dispatcher uses the RouteSelect feature on the Web site to find the fastest route to the accident. By typing in the accident location as the trip origin, and the address of the nearest hospital as the destination, the dispatcher can give drivers the best route to that hospital even before they leave for the accident.

On the commercial side, delivery fleet managers no longer have to stand by helplessly while their trucks are stuck in traffic. Their drivers can be given directions skirting the city's heaviest congestion before the drivers even hit it. The fleet managers can also notify customers when deliveries are delayed and when the truck will get there.

Fleet dispatchers use the Web site to plan routes for delivery vehicles or ambulances.

Behind the scenes

Traffic data for the system is collected at two thousand intersections with sensors buried in the pavement and closed-circuit televisions (CCTVs). In addition, 120 taxis equipped with global positioning system (GPS) receivers collect traffic data twenty-four hours a day.

All the data is sent to a Traffic Operations Centre, where it is stored in six servers running an Oracle database. Spatial Database Engine (SDE) makes this data available spatially for display on digital maps provided by Korea Automotive Technology Institute.

The data is then processed, which produces speed estimates for Seoul's roads, intersections, and bridges. The Traffic Operations Centre uses this data, along with information about accidents and road work, to calculate travel routes with an Advanced Traveler Information System from the Korea Highway Corporation. These estimates, which are updated on the display every ten minutes, appear as red (jammed), yellow (slow), and green (fast) lines on the roads. The data, continuously viewed by traffic analysts at the Centre, is made available to the public over the Internet at www.kortic.or.kr.

In the system's Traffic Operations Centre, operators use GIS maps to view data about Seoul's traffic.

How traffic is analyzed

Analysts at the Traffic Control Centre use custom applications programmed with Microsoft Visual C++® for map display, and ANSI C for traffic data analysis. Working with both, they are able to monitor traffic speeds and investigate and react to incidents.

At night, as commuters leave the city, the streets on the maps turn mainly green and yellow. When traffic stops at this hour, and the streets suddenly turn red, analysts use the system to view the area from the closest CCTV. In some cases, this will tell them why traffic is stopped and they can send a tow truck or an ambulance. If no CCTV is close, they can use the maps to locate mobile communication vehicles. Using two-way radios, the driver of the closest one can give them more information about the situation.

RTSA has upgraded the application since 1998 with MapObjects and Delphi™ software.

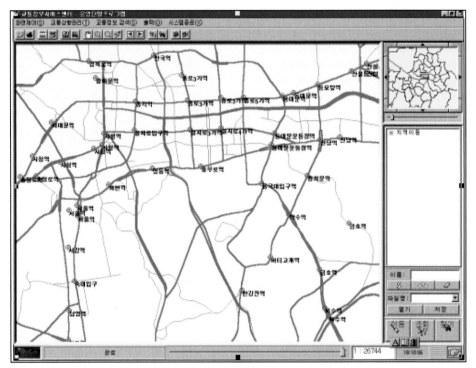

When CCTV data is unavailable, analysts use maps and two-way radios to gather information about an incident.

A faster future

Researchers at the Road Traffic Information Centre are working with Korean automobile manufacturers like KIA to provide drivers with current traffic information and routing services through in-vehicle navigation systems by 2003.

Another project is providing the data and maps to Korea's police and fire departments, both of which already use SDE. These agencies will integrate the system used by the Traffic Operations Centre's operators.

In the future, the system will integrate signals from cellular phones with the maps to provide locations of cars involved in emergency situations. As in other countries, cellular technology can be part of a personal "Mayday system" to send a signal when an airbag deploys. This service could save lives when drivers are disabled, out of sight, or unconscious.

Plans are already in motion to duplicate this privately funded traffic system for other major Korean cities—Pusan, Kwangju, Daegu, and Daejon—to move people, goods, and services more freely and quickly.

Analysts view real-time traffic on PC monitors and on wall displays. They can view the entire region or specific streets.

Hardware

Two HP 420s for data processing and GIS

PC PSDN server (provides traffic data to public)

Web server

Image-processing server

Data-gathering server (manages raw data from loop detectors and other agencies)

Statistics-processing server

Software

Spatial Database Engine (SDE)

Oracle

Advanced Traveler Information System

Data

Real-time traffic data

Roads

Administrative areas

Topographical features

Lakes and rivers

Raster backgrounds

Traffic regulation data

Acknowledgments

Thanks to Bisi Lee, project manager, CADLAND, Inc., South Korea.

Books from ESRI Press

Enterprise GIS for Energy Companies
A volume of case studies showing how electric and gas utilities use geographic information systems to manage their facilities more cost effectively, find new market opportunities, and better serve their customers.   ISBN 1-879102-48-X

Transportation GIS
From monitoring rail systems and airplane noise levels, to making bus routes more efficient and improving roads, this book describes how geographic information systems have emerged as the tool of choice for transportation planners.   ISBN 1-879102-41-1

Getting to Know ArcView GIS
A colorful, nontechnical introduction to GIS technology and ArcView GIS software, this workbook comes with a working ArcView GIS demonstration copy. Follow the book's scenario-based exercises or work through them using the CD and learn how to do your own ArcView GIS project.   ISBN 1-879102-46-3

Serving Maps on the Internet
Take an insider's look at how today's forward-thinking organizations distribute map-based information via the Internet. Case studies cover a range of applications for Internet Map Server technology from ESRI. This book should interest anyone who wants to publish geospatial data on the World Wide Web.   ISBN 1-879102-52-8

Managing Natural Resources with GIS
Find out how GIS technology helps people design solutions to such pressing challenges as wildfires, urban blight, air and water degradation, species endangerment, disaster mitigation, coastline erosion, and public education. The experiences of public and private organizations provide real-world examples.   ISBN 1-879102-53-6

Zeroing In: Geographic Information Systems at Work in the Community
In twelve "tales from the digital map age," this book shows how people use GIS in their daily jobs. An accessible and engaging introduction to GIS for anyone who deals with geographic information.   ISBN 1-879102-50-1

ArcView GIS Means Business
Written for business professionals, this book is a behind-the-scenes look at how some of America's most successful companies have used desktop GIS technology. The book is loaded with full-color illustrations and comes with a trial copy of ArcView GIS software and a GIS tutorial.   ISBN 1-879102-51-X

ARC Macro Language: Developing Menus and Macros with AML
ARC Macro Language (AML™) software gives you the power to tailor workstation ARC/INFO software's geoprocessing operations to specific applications. This workbook teaches AML in the context of accomplishing practical workstation ARC/INFO tasks, and presents both basic and advanced techniques.   ISBN 1-879102-18-8

Understanding GIS: The ARC/INFO Method (workstation ARC/INFO)
A hands-on introduction to geographic information system technology. Designed primarily for beginners, this classic text guides readers through a complete GIS project in ten easy-to-follow lessons.
ISBN 1-879102-00-5

ESRI Press publishes a growing list of GIS-related books. Ask for these books at your local bookstore or order by calling **1-800-447-9778.** *You can also shop online at* **www.esri.com/gisstore.** *Outside the United States, contact your local ESRI distributor.*

ESRI Press ▪ 380 New York Street ▪ Redlands, California 92373-8100